'Matthew Crampton has taken a fresh look at the worlds of slavery and emigration. He's unearthed some fascinating stories and, crucially, added folk song to let us hear from those whose voices are usually silenced. Songs give such a distinct perspective on history – and this book gives us an elegant, vital insight into human suffering and survival.'
Cerys Matthews

PRAISE FOR HUMAN CARGO – THE SHOW

'Beautiful, powerful, poignant and informative.'
Ilyaz Hajat, The Refugee Council

'A privilege to see this wonderful performance, using folk songs from different cultures ... to dramatise some of the worst stains on human history. I can't recommend Human Cargo highly enough.'
Robin Beste

HUMAN CARGO

Stories and songs of emigration,
slavery and transportation

Matthew Crampton

Muddler Books

Matthew Crampton is a writer and folk singer.
He lives in London and likes to go fishing.

humancargo.co.uk
matthewcrampton.com

First published in 2016 by Muddler Books.
© 2016 Matthew Crampton
Set in 11/16 New Baskerville
Designed by Matthew Crampton

ISBN 978-0-9561361-2-1

Illustrations in this book come from the collections of
John Foreman and the author. Credits for song lyrics
appear in the Index of Songs.

for
Marie Lasenby

CONTENTS

INTRODUCTION

F leets of flimsy craft try to cross the southern Mediterranean. Many fail. Each day brings fresh news of this saga, with its cast list of evil traffickers, opportunist politicians, diligent rescuers and, within it all, families striving to stay human while plunged into indignity.

This story is not new. Tales of trafficking and transportation flow through history. For Europeans they reached a height in the 18th and 19th centuries, when economic progress swept poor flotsam to new worlds hungry for their labour. Some paid their passage, others sat in chains, all swelled a tide of human cargo.

Most of us have heard of the Middle Passage of slaves from Africa to the Americas. We've seen that diagram of black bodies packed like sardines into the hold. This is considered, rightly, the depth of horror. But many others went through their own middle passage, whether as slaves, indentured servants, convicts or emigrants. Stuck in the hold, tossed about in a cramped world of pain, fear and tedium, this journey marked an irrevocable change in their life, usually for the worse. Human cargo was seldom happy cargo.

Today, smartphones can take us right into migrant boats. We can perch among the bodies and hear the groans. But how do we put a face on migrants of the past? How do we attend to those who were mostly illiterate or excluded from the narrative?

And if we could hear these past travellers, how might their experience help us attend to those today in terrified transit?

Some personal accounts exist from the 1700s, more from later on. This book draws upon these self-published tales, including Olaudah Equiano's rare description of a slave boat from the slave's perspective, Peter Williamson's story of being kidnapped in

Aberdeen, James M'Lean's life as an American sailor pressed into the Royal Navy and Robert Whyte's passage on an Irish coffin ship.

But these were survivors, and successful, and men. What of the others on board? We may not hear directly from them, but we can listen, opaquely, through folk song. Thousands of lyrics survive in ballad and broadside, from the direst of doggerel to straight, unmannered poetry. And there are songs not written then, but passed from mouth to ear until 20th century collectors noted them down. Folk songs are hardly history; they're not facts or quantifiable. But the songs that persisted did so because different people, time and again, were touched by them and wanted to sing them for themselves. So they're a valid collective memory, giving voice to the silent.

The songs appear here without melody, just as those early broadsheets arrived on the street, crudely printed, crudely sold. Being popular entertainment, they tend to be direct in their emotions. They skip easily from horror to romance, from sweetness to violence – often cloaking terrible deeds with jaunty manner. In so doing, they help leaven what might otherwise become a catalogue of misery.

Among the old stories and songs I've sprinkled some modern testimony: snapshots of human cargo in the 21st century. Where past tales surprise and old songs engage, today's stories help you shudder. They're horrible. And in their similarity to the past, for cruelty remains constant, they bring that past alive.

In late 2014 I was asked to create a words-and-music show for the Harwich Shanty Festival in Eastern England. *Human Cargo* seemed a canny device for linking songs with different themes: slavery, emigration, convict transportation, the press gang, Barbary pirates and the Highland Clearances. And so it proved. But with 2015 came those dark reports from the Southern Med. Suddenly the notion of human cargo gained sharper relevance.

With my colleagues Chris Hayes, Daisy Johnson and Jan North – singing together as *The London Lubbers* – we prepared our songs for Harwich, where we opened the festival in October 2015. The show touched a nerve. We repeated it in London as a benefit for The Refugee Council. It touched more nerves – and led to this book, which enabled me to delve deeper.

The book divides roughly into two. The first part tells of those who had no choice in entering the hold: African slaves bound for Jamaica, English children kidnapped to become indentured servants in Virginia, Melanesian coolies heading for plantations in Queensland, white Europeans seized for the North African slave markets, Irish political prisoners exported to Virginia, Hebrideans cleared to Canada, landlubbers pressed into the Royal Navy and English petty criminals transported to New South Wales.

The second part considers those who chose to go, even if duped or under duress. Here we meet European emigrants seeking a new life across the Atlantic, farm lads who took the King's Shilling to join the army, prospectors heading to Australia for gold, and those 'crimped' or enticed to join the merchant navy.

The book offers no more than a glimpse into their lives, but time and again we meet that same cast list. On one side the duplicitous traffickers, corrupt authorities and petty bullies. On the other, desperate folk who've been tricked, trapped or have simply run out of options.

If you want to look further, you might start with the reading I reference at the end. There's an Index of Songs. If any songs touch you, why not seek out recordings, perhaps even sing them for yourself?

Today's refugee crisis demands witness – and action – but is hard to grasp. Story and song won't solve the problems, but they can help find a way in.

ACKNOWLEDGEMENTS

One of the great pleasures of creating this book was time spent at the Camden Town home of John Foreman – 'the Broadsheet King', singer, storyteller, printer and publisher – a noble iconoclast, living spirit of the Music Hall and excellent provider of tea and cake. Within the many thousand volumes piled neatly, and precariously, throughout his house, I found most of the illustrations for this book. Thank you John for so generously sharing them with me.

I was lucky to have expert assistance in reviewing the text – Mike Sumner, Susan Hitch, Pippa Eldridge from Daunt Books and Rachel Elliot from the English Folk Dance and Song Society (EFDSS) – though I bear responsibility for any mistakes I slipped past them or added later. Anna MacDonald kindly took pains to check the Gaelic is correct. I appreciate the publishing advice of Will Hammond, Sarah Rigby and Anna Webber. I'd also like to thank Cerys Matthews, Maurice Wren of The Refugee Council, Steve Kamlish and Marie Lasenby. Finally, I thank Chris Hayes, Daisy Johnson and Jan North for their help in developing, over many happy evenings of roast chicken and rehearsal, the show of *Human Cargo*, from which this book arose.

BLACK SHEEP

Oh, was you ever on the Congo River?
  Blow boys blow
Yes I've been down the Congo River
  Blow me bully boys blow
The Congo she's a mighty river
  Blow boys blow
Where the fever makes the white man shiver
  Blow me bully boys blow

Beware, beware the Bight of Benin
  Blow boys blow
Where one comes out for forty that goes in
  Blow me bully boys blow
A Yankee ship come down the river
  Blow boys blow
Her mast and yards they shone like silver
  Blow me bully boys blow

And how do I know she's a Yankee clipper?
  Blow boys blow
By the blood and guts that runs from her scupper
  Blow me bully boys blow
And who do you think was master of her?
  Blow boys blow
Oh Shanghai Brown, that Yankee lover
  Blow me bully boys blow

Who do you think was first mate of her?
  Blow boys blow
Why, Shanghai Brown, the sailor robber
  Blow me bully boys blow
What do you think we had for supper?
  Blow boys blow
Oh, handspike hash and a roll in the scuppers
  Blow me bully boys blow

What do you think we had for cargo?
  Blow boys blow
Why, black sheep that have run the embargo
  Blow me bully boys blow
It's blow today and blow tomorrow
  Blow boys blow
We'll blow this hell-ship all in sorrow
  Blow me bully boys blow

PART ONE

Taken with Violence

This is a tale of cargo. But not your usual cargo, such as pine from Nova Scotia, silk from Bombay or coal from Newcastle. This is about HUMAN CARGO.

In the 18th and 19th centuries, the oceans teemed with shiploads of people, taken against their will and transported to strange, distant shores. Let's name some of them. PETER WILLIAMSON, at the age of eight, was seized off the streets of Aberdeen and sold into servitude in South Carolina. CATHERINE MACPHEE was cleared from her Hebridean home and forced by her landlord onto a boat for Nova Scotia. Petty thief JOHN LAUSON, 18, was transported to America for 14 years while frail 82-year-old DOROTHY HANDLYN was sent to New South Wales in chains, for perjury.

OLAUDAH EQUIANO was viciously enslaved as a child in Africa, then carried in chains to Barbados to learn a thing or two about sugar production.

These are some of the millions of people carried in despair across the sea. They may have been cargo to their carriers, but they were humans. And humans survive by story and song.

SPIRITED AWAY

I n 1757 a Scotsman called Peter Williamson published his life story. He'd had an interesting life – and he needed money. This is how his tale began:

> *Know, therefore, that I was born within ten Miles of the Town of Aberdeen if not of rich, yet of reputable Parents. I was sent to live with an Aunt at Aberdeen where, at eight Years of Age, playing on the quay with my Companions, being of a stout robust Constitution, I was taken Notice of by two Fellows belonging to a Vessel in the Harbour, employed by some of the worthy Merchants of the Town, in that villainous and execrable Practice called Kidnapping – stealing young Children from their Parents and selling them as Slaves in the Plantations abroad. I was easily cajoled on board the Ship by them. In about a Month's Time the Ship set sail for America.*

This happened a lot back then. Children would vanish. So would adults. Those gone were said to have been *spirited away*, but the spirits that took them were not ghosts. They were paid traffickers. They might be rogues or idlers, they might be yeomen or doctors; even the mayor of Bristol was once suspected.

The most famous story of spiriting away was Robert Louis Stevenson's 1751 novel *Kidnapped:* 17 year old David Balfour, newly orphaned, seeks help from his uncle, an evil man who steals the boy's fortune and has him kidnapped aboard a ship to be sold in the Carolinas.

In modern times we have such spirits too: the young men in Romania who talk sweet to girls then lure them away to brothels in Huddersfield, or the Bangladeshi gangmasters gathering slaves to build World Cup stadia in Qatar.

Today's Qatar was then the Carolinas. The new American colonies needed labour, however it could be procured. As early as 1645, Parliament banned 'diverse lewd persons who in a barbarous manner steal away little children'. But this had little effect. Nor did later laws, for trafficking was, and remains, a profitable business. As Peter Williamson continued:

> *When landed at Philadelphia, the Capital of Pennsylvania, the Captain had soon People enough who came to buy us. He making the most of his villainous Loading sold us at about 16 pounds per Head. What became of my unhappy Companions, I never knew; but it was my Lot to be sold for the Term of seven Years to one of my Countrymen, who had in his Youth undergone the same Fate as myself; having been kidnapped from St. Johnstone in Scotland.*

Williamson was sold for seven years' indenture – a form of slavery. Like the majority of Europeans landing in colonial America, he had no rights: he was valued less than some livestock, and could be bought or sold as his master wished. This didn't match the evil of permanently enslaving a race, as with the African slave trade. Even so, half such European servants did not survive their term of indenture.

Some came voluntarily, accepting a lump sum for their servitude. But those spirited away received no bounty. Little wonder people in Britain were so scared of being kidnapped. In the poorer quarters of London, to accuse someone of being a spirit was a good way to raise a riot.

There are ballads from as far back as the 17th century, which boast of a harried husband taking revenge by having his wife abducted to Virginia. One famous one was called *A Net for a Night Raven* or *A Trap for a Scold*. In this version, titled *The Scolding Wife*, 'an honest man and a weaver' decides to sell his spouse into indentured servitude for £50. He tricks her aboard the kidnap vessel by pretending to be emigrating himself. Though such abductions did take place, the song likely reflects male fantasy more than common practice. And, typically for a folk song, it treats human cruelty with jaunty measure.

The Scolding Wife

There lives a man into this toon
An honest man and a weaver,
He had a wife and a scolding wife
And he could not live beside her.

He's done him doon to a ship's captain,
Says, 'Buy ye any women?
I have a fine Italian wench
Just fitting for a seaman.

'It's fifty pounds I ask for her,
And not a penny lacking.'
'Ye'll bring her down to me this night
And ye'll receive your asking.'

He's done him doon to his scolding wife,
'My sweetheart and my honey,
I've bargained with a ship's captain
For the lands o' brave Virginny.

'And all that I do ask of thee
Is to go to shipboard wi' me,
And a bottle o' good liquor strong
I shall bestow upon thee.'

He set his foot upon the deck,
'Come here to me, my honey.'
He set his foot upon the pier,
'Goodnight and joy be with ye.'

When she did see that she was betrayed,
'My sweetheart and my honey,
Gin ye but take me back again,
I never shall offend thee.'

'Fare you well, my scolding wife,
I wish you wind and weather,
And nine months sailing on the sea
Before you find a harbour.'

The captain's called this man aside
And paid him down his money,
She got another husband there
In the lands of brave Virginny.

It's all that I do say to you,
Don't nag your husband, honey,
For fear they take the fifty pounds
When they grow scant o' money.

TRAFFICKED

In 1904 a young Japanese woman called Minami Haru was persuaded she could earn good money by working in a restaurant in Singapore. To get there she boarded a ship in Kuchinotsu harbour, though she was surprised to be taken to the ship surreptitiously in the middle of the night. Once on board, Haru found herself trapped within the hold, where she spent four weeks living off bread crusts. Reaching Singapore, she was forced to work as a prostitute. This was a typical journey for Japanese peasants tricked into slavery within the richer cities of Southeast Asia. In 1905 a Fukuoka newspaper described how 48 Japanese teenagers were discovered in the coal bunker of a Norwegian vessel heading for Hong Kong.

Chinese merchants also trafficked women and children from Vietnam, again to Hong Kong, Canton and Shanghai. They often used British and German steamers, where the best hiding place was amongst the coal. A 1907 Haiphong newspaper talked of children being knocked out with chloroform, then spirited away on fishing boats. Usually, these children were expected to work in brothels as servants or prostitutes. There was a tradition of childless older prostitutes 'adopting' an infant as their own, teaching them the ways of the brothel so the child might support them in their old age.

In 1932 the League of Nations published its *Commission of Enquiry into Traffic in Women and Children in the East*. This included a personal account of the abduction of a woman from Vietnam, who would then have been described as Annamite:

In Hanoi, the Commission had the opportunity of meeting an Annamite woman who had been kidnapped in Haiphong, taken to China and sold there. In 1922, when she was 18 years old,

*another Annamite woman of about 40 approached her in
Haiphong and suggested that they should go to Nai-chang to buy
areca nuts, which were cheap there. The girl consented and went
on board the woman's sampan ... When she awoke the next
morning, the woman was not there but there were four Chinese
men who bound her arms and feet and threatened her with
knives to keep silence. She was taken ashore to a cave in which
were five kidnapped Annamite girls. The men put all the girls
on a junk which travelled only in the night, the girls being taken
ashore and hidden in the daytime. After nine days, they were
landed and made to walk for several hours to a little village,
where all the girls were put up for sale in a kind of market. The
witness was sold for 236 dollars (silver) to a Chinese farmer ...
About a year after her arrival she gave birth to a child, but, as it
was a girl and the man wanted a son, he killed the new-born
baby by strangling it.*

Here is a similar story, but more recent:

*'It was only four years ago when a young man from Skopje came
into my father's shop. He was very polite and well dressed ... his
name was Damir and he spoke of the famous cities he often
visited ... he said he worked for a modelling agency that looks for
pretty girls like I was.' So said Maria, a 17-year-old Albanian
who was trafficked into sex slavery in Italy in 1998. Travelling
by boat from Durrës to Bari, she thought she was going to work
as a model, but gradually she realised her travelling conditions
heralded a worse fate. 'It was the first time I saw the sea and my
first time in a ship. It seemed very big and beautiful. We followed
Damir, who had our tickets and travel documents. He spoke
with an official and gave him something before we went into the
ship and down many stairs. I thought we were near the engine –
the smell of oil was very strong, also rotten food and the smell of*

clothes not washed in a long time. He said for our safety he must lock the door but will return in the morning ... we wished to talk about the handsome men we are going to meet and how the girls at home will be jealous, but the bad smells and moving ship made me very sick ... the next morning we arrived in Bari. Damir took us to a house where the streets are dirty and we saw beggars and even rats during the day ... the polite young man from my father's shop grabbed my arm and said something very bad in Albanian. He hit me on the face ... I did not understand what had happened. I heard other girls screaming. And then he raped me. Then the other men came in and did the same ... he said this was modelling that we must do for anyone.'

A FLEXIBLE WORKFORCE

Today's lovers of zero-hours contracts and flexible workforces would no doubt praise the means by which the rich sourced labour in the 18th century. They'd argue that voluntary indenture enabled poor Brits to 'get on their bikes' and follow opportunities in expanding markets, where kindly employers would even pay their passage to these new opportunities.

In practice, of course, life wasn't so sweet. First, you had to survive the journey by sea. Then you had to survive the work, with no rights over the hours you laboured or the conditions in which you were kept. Fall too ill to work and you'd likely be cast out to die. Most colonial servants died in bondage, but if you did survive the term, you'd probably emerge landless and poor, with little chance of affording passage back to Britain. Your best bet then was to sign on for another seven years.

The newspapers of colonial America often featured runaway ads, placed by masters hunting their servants and slaves. This one is typical of the period.

Maryland Gazette, Annapolis, November 7 1745

FIVE PISTOLES REWARD. RAN away from the subscriber, in Fairfax County, an English indented Servant Woman, named Elizabeth Bushup, about 23 Years of Age, of a low Stature, fair Skin, black Eyes, black Hair, a Scar on her Breast, and loves Drink; had on when she went away, a Calico Gown and Petticoat, a Pair of Stays, a Hoop Coat, a black Furr'd Hat, a Pair of Calimanco Shoes, a Muslin Apron, and several other Things too tedious to mention. It is suspected she was carried away, by Capt. Tipple's Boatswain, from Potowmack River to Patuxent, where the Ship lies, or that he has left her at the Mouth of the River. Whoever takes up the said Servant, and brings her to her Master, shall have Five Pistoles Reward, besides what the Law allows, and Five Pistoles more if it can be proved that the said Boatswain conceals her.

GERRARD ALEXANDER

Today's indentures match those of centuries ago. Here are two tales of bonded labour in India from 2004:

My name is Munni Devi. I've been working in the quarry for a long, long time, many years. Maybe twenty years, maybe more. I'm not sure. My husband died while working there, and now I have to work there myself. Life is tough. I've taken a loan because of which I'm a slave to the person from whom I took it. And now the situation is getting even worse. I'm in debt. I can't work that much, and he threatens to throw me out of my house. I've been working under the same contractor, and I've taken one loan and now it seems to have doubled to become two loans. My original loan was for 9,000 rupees ($200) and I've been trying to repay it for a long, long time. It just seems to be increasing.

My name is Rambho Kumar and I am eleven years old. A man named Shankar and the owner of the loom came one day to my house and gave 700 rupees ($15) for me. They told my parents that they were going to educate me and make me do some work. I was crying and saying that I didn't want to go there. They said they're going to give me money. He'll send money home and then after some time I can come back. (Later, after a very long time, they told me I'm not going to be able to go back home ever.) After two days I reached the loom and they made me sit down. They told me to learn how to use the loom. My hand got cut, and the owner and his brother shut my eyes and put my finger in boiling oil and said, 'Now it's all right, now you get back to work'. If I made any mistake, the loom owner used to take a stick and beat me. I kept asking the loom owner when I would go to school, and he kept telling me, 'There is not school for you. You will spend time weaving carpets.' I used to work from four in the morning till eleven in the night. At about ten in the morning we used to get our first meal, which was not good. And that was all we did during the day: weaving carpets, eating food, and going to sleep.

WHITE SLAVES, BARBARY SLAVERS

June 19th 1631 was like any other day in the remote Irish village of Baltimore in West Cork. The fishing boats returned from hunting shoals of pilchard. Villagers gutted and barrelled the catch, pressing the fish to collect its rich oil. Then they went to bed. As night fell, they didn't notice two strange vessels drop anchor barely a musket shot's distance from the harbour.

Before dawn the villagers were awoken by shouting. There was a smell of burning thatch, then the sound of screams. Strange figures were running through the village: 200 armed corsairs, forcing men, women and children into chains. These were Barbary pirates 1,000 miles from their home in Algiers. They'd come to source product for the slave markets of North Africa. 108 inhabitants of Baltimore were taken to become galley slaves, labourers and concubines. Barely a handful returned. The others faced short, terrible lives; galley slaves, for example, were never allowed ashore and worked like animals until they died.

This was no isolated incident. During the 1620s and 1630s alone, it's reckoned that 7,000 English people were abducted by pirates, both from ships and from raids, mostly in parts of Devon and Cornwall. Much worse hit were Italy, Portugal and Spain. Indeed, one historian reckons that over a million

WHITE SLAVERY IN THE EAST.

ABDUCTION OF A WHITE GIRL BY SLAVE-HUNTERS.

Europeans became Arab slaves between the 1500s and 1800s. Off the rough north coast of the Spanish island of Mallorca there's a cave in the cliffs, only accessible from the sea. Sail close and you notice strange man-made steps leading up to it; Arab pirates used the cave as a holding pen for captured white slaves. Evidence of a nasty, little-known trade.

But it wasn't just Barbary pirates who kidnapped poor Irish people. In 1653, two decades after the attack on Baltimore, Oliver Cromwell gave licence to English merchants to transport 8,000 'natural Irish' to America. They could seize pretty much anyone they wished along the coast, so serving three imperial aims: removing Catholics, creating space for English settlers and providing cheap labour for the colonies.

THE

CRUELTIES

OF THE

ALGERINE PIRATES,

SHEWING THE

Present Dreadful State

OF THE

ENGLISH SLAVES,

AND OTHER EUROPEANS

AT

ALGIERS AND TUNIS ;

WITH THE

HORRID BARBARITIES

INFLICTED ON CHRISTIAN MARINERS SHIPWRECKED

ON THE

NORTH WESTERN COAST OF AFRICA AND CARRIED INTO PERPETUAL SLAVERY

AUTHENTICATED

By Mr. JACKSON, of Morocco; Mr. MACGILL, Merchant

AND

By Capt. WALTER CROKER,

Of His Majesty's Sloop *Wizard*

LONDON

PRINTED FOR W. HONE, 55, FLEET-STREET

1816   Price Sixpence

Fear of Muslim pirates persisted well into the 19th century. In 1815 a British naval captain called Walter Croker took his sloop *Wizard* into Algiers, where he found, to his horror, a sad band of Christian slaves. This prompted a popular pamphlet, which started with some reflections on the recent success of Abolition:

> *There is a fashion in humanity as in everything else; this may be observed even in its daily exercise in common life, but as exemplifed in political and national practice, it is strikingly apparent. The people of Great Britain speak with horror of the Negro Slave Trade, and attend to its manifold miseries with the genuine feelings of men and of christians, yet the same people hear, as affairs of constant recurrence and with perfect apathy, that thousands of the civilized inhabitants of the shores of the Mediterranean, of both sexes, and of every age, are dragged into the direst captivity by the most cruel and blood-thirsty barbarians upon record!*

'Authenticated' by Captain Croker, the prose took purple pleasure in detailing the hideous excesses of the heathen pirates:

> *When Captain Croker enquired into the particulars of the capture of these wretched people, he found, on the authority of all the Consuls in Algiers, that they were a part of three hundred and fifty-seven, who had been taken by two Algerine pirates, carrying English Colours, by which stratagem they were decoyed within their reach. Landed at Bona, these unhappy people had been driven to Algiers like a herd of cattle. Such as were no longer able to walk had been tied on Mules, and many who had become still more enfeebled, were murdered without ceremony! On their journey fifty-nine expired! One youth fell dead the very moment they brought him to the feet of the Dey; and within six days from their arrival at Algiers, nearly seventy men were delivered by death from the inhumanity of these monsters in human shape!*

The pamphlet asked why Europe, which once 'exhausted itself in absurd expeditions', presumably the Crusades, could not now be roused to wipe out a few bands of pirates; and hinted corrupt elements in Britain, as bad as the African slavers, were at work:

> *That there may exist Interests which such an alteration would affect, cannot be doubted, and they may even possess partizans in a British House of Commons ... Others, as in the Negro Slave Trade, will affect incredulity and all manner of unbelief of the sufferings stated.*

The Royal Navy loved to liberate English slaves from pirates. Once rescued, the captives would be brought home to parade through the streets, still wearing their chains and tattered clothes. Onlookers would sing *Rule, Britannia! Britannia rule the waves. Britons never will be slaves.* And they also liked to sing songs about chasing those pirates...

The Coasts of High Barbary

Look ahead, look astern, look the weather in the lee,
> *Blow high! Blow low! And so sailed we.*
I see a wreck to windward and a lofty ship to lee,
> *A sailing down all on the coast of High Barbary*

O are you a pirate or a man-o-war, cried we
> *Blow high! Blow low! And so sailed we.*
O no! I'm not a pirate but a man-o-war, cried he
> *A sailing down all on the coasts of High Barbary*

We'll back up our topsails and heave our vessel to,
> *Blow high! Blow low! And so sailed we.*

For we have got some letters to be carried home by you.
  A sailing down all on the coasts of High Barbary

For broadside, for broadside they fought all on the main,
  Blow high! Blow low! And so sailed we.
Until at last the frigate shot the pirate's mast away.
  A sailing down all on the coasts of High Barbary

For quarters! For quarters! The saucy pirates cried,
  Blow high! Blow low! And so sailed we.
The quarters that we showed them was to sink them in the tide.
  A sailing down all on the coasts of High Barbary

But O it was a cruel sight and grieved us full sore
  Blow high! Blow low! And so sailed we.
To see them all a drowning as they tried to swim to shore
  A sailing down all on the coasts of High Barbary

So there were white slaves. There still are. When we read recently of a British Asian gang grooming a young white girl in Aylesbury market, passing her round for sex, there were echoes of the old broadsheet tales of Barbary pirates. But the vast majority of slaves then, as now, were not white.

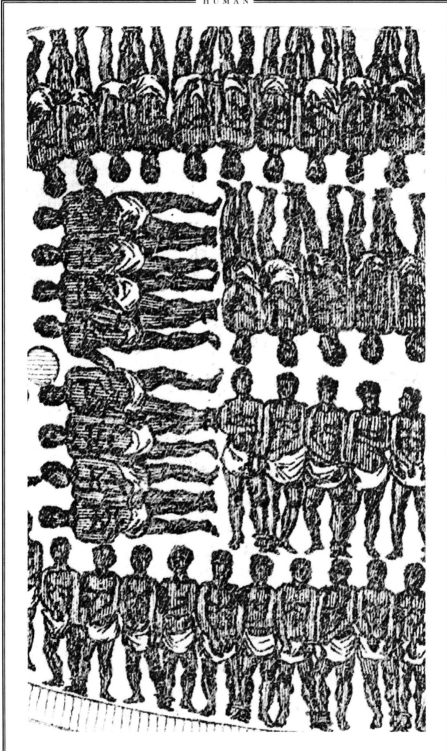

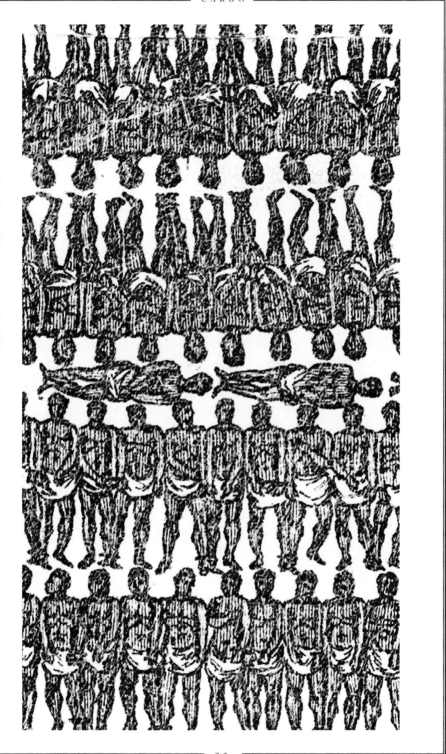

THE ZONG

Saturday 18th August 1781. A ship called the *Zong* leaves the port of Accra in Ghana. Its destination is Jamaica, across the Atlantic. The *Zong* is small, only 107 tons, with a crew of seventeen. It's a slave ship which, for its size, should carry no more than 200 slaves. But the *Zong* is crammed with 442 slaves, more than twice its capacity.

The captain, Luke Collingwood, knows little of navigation or command. He's a surgeon. But he knows about slaves, for he's just spent weeks selecting cargo from the holding pens ashore in Ghana. His job was to assess each captive's commercial value. Those he rejected were then seen as unsellable by their African handlers and usually killed on the spot.

So here is the *Zong*: a small boat, under-crewed, over-laden, with no proper captain. What could go wrong?

29th November, three and a half months later. After a chaotic crossing, the ship has overshot Jamaica. It needs a further ten days to beat back to port, but it's only got four days' water. 62 slaves have already died, along with several crew. The captain's sick, as are many of the hands and most of the cargo. All the slaves might well die before they reach port.

That's a problem, for no cargo means no pay. The slaves are insured, for £30 a head, but the insurance doesn't cover natural death such as starving or dehydration. The crew gather to decide what to do. After a while, someone has an idea: why not jettison a portion of cargo to save the rest? But for this to work under maritime law, they must jettison valid cargo; ie, live slaves.

Even to hardened slavers, the idea must have been monstrous. Yet they soon agreed, and that afternoon they slung 54 women and children through the cabin windows. Two days later they jettisoned 42 male slaves, then a further 36. Ten more Africans jumped defiantly into the sea of their own volition. By now many sharks swam happily behind the ship.

At this point it started raining heavily and the crew were able to collect six casks of water, enough for eleven days. So the slaughter had not even been needed. On 22nd December 1781, the *Zong* arrived at Black River Jamaica. Of its original 442 slaves, 208 remained. These were sold for around £36 each.

When news reached Britain, the ship's owners in Liverpool rushed to claim compensation for the ejected slaves. The insurers refused payment, prompting a court case which, in effect, ruled that the owners were within their rights to claim – it being a matter of civil insurance, not murder – but crew mistakes meant this particular claim was void. Judge Mansfield said that 'the Case of Slaves was the same as if Horses had been thrown overboard.'

Those fine houses you see in Liverpool and Bristol would not have been built if the nation had softened, too early, its regard for the rights of cargo owners.

THE LOADING OF THE CARGO

I n 1773 Henry Smeathman, a British naturalist, stopped by a slave port while collecting insects along the coast. The port was Bance Island in the estuary of the Sierra Leone River, one of West Africa's most active trading posts – where half the white population died each year. Its fortress had holding pens for slaves, ready to be collected by slave ships on the Triangular Trade: the geometric flow of guns to Africa, slaves to America and molasses to Europe.

Smeathman was not prepared for what he saw. Here he describes the ships filling their holds with slaves:

> *What a scene of misery and distress is a full slaved ship in the rains. The clanking of chains, the groans of the sick and the stench of the whole ... two or three slaves thrown overboard each day dying of fever flux, measles, worms all together. All the day the chains rattling or the sound of the armourer riveting some poor devil just arrived in galling heavy irons. Here the doctor dressing sores, wounds and ulcers, or cramming the men with medicines and another standing over them with a cat (-o'-nine tails) to make them swallow.*

No More Auction Block For Me

No more auction block for me,
No more, no more.
No more auction block for me,
Many thousand gone.

No more peck of corn for me,
No more, no more.
No more peck of corn for me,
Many thousand gone.

No more pint of salt for me,
No more, no more.
No more pint of salt for me,
Many thousand gone.

No more driver's lash for me,
No more, no more.
No more driver's lash for me,
Many thousand gone.

GHOST SHIPS

As twilight fell on Thursday 30th December 1824, the British ship *Ascension* was busy heading back to Europe from Brazil when, through the darkness, her lookout spotted something in the distance. It appeared to be a capsized ship. Her captain ordered the *Ascension* to change course and soon they found a floating wreck with figures holding onto a floating piece of mast. Little could be done as night fell, so the ship stayed close to the spot, helped by calm weather. As soon as there was enough light, the *Ascension* sent out two boats, which collected 31 survivors, all Africans, and learnt what had happened. This was a slave boat which had run into trouble. As it foundered, the slavers had made their escape, leaving their cargo to be drowned. At this point the rescuers heard knocking from within the upturned hull. The *Ascension's* carpenters cut through the thick wood and rescued 10 more Africans who had survived on the little air left within. Some 200 slaves were thought to have died in the wreck. Stories of this ghost ship soon spread along the Brazilian coast.

Two centuries later in January 2015, a journalist reported:

> *The Italian Coast Guard was last night towing the second unmanned ship containing hundreds of migrants to appear off its coast this week into port. The so-called 'ghost ships' are a worrying new trend as human traffickers exploit desperate refugees bidding for a new life in Europe. The Lebanese vessel*

Ezadeen, which was discovered with about 450 passengers on board, is registered as a livestock vessel. But even cattle are not left to cross dangerous high seas in mid-winter with no crew and the vessel on autopilot. The practice of using 'ghost ships' – filling rust buckets with refugees, pointing the vessel towards Italy and then fleeing with the passengers' life-savings – appears to be a worrying new development in human trafficking. 'They purchase unseaworthy vessels for $100,000 to $150,000 (£65,000 to £97,000) and then fill them with hundreds of migrants, mainly Syrian nationals, who pay $6,000 each for the crossing from the Turkish coast to Europe,' said Admiral Pettorino. He told the Adnkronos news agency that the criminals were netting up to $5m per trip and therefore 'had no hesitation about jumping ship, given the profit margins'.

The Slave's Lament

It was in sweet Senegal that my foes did me enthral
*   For the lands of Virginia, -ginia, O.*
Torn from that lovely shore, and must never see it more;
*   And alas! I am weary, weary O.*

All on that charming coast is no bitter snow and frost,
*   Like the lands of Virginia, -ginia, O:*
Their streams for ever flow, and their flowers for ever blow,
*   And alas! I am weary, weary O.*

The burden I must bear, while the cruel scourge I fear,
*   In the lands of Virginia, -ginia, O;*
And I think on friends most dear, with the bitter, bitter tear,
*   And alas! I am weary, weary O.*

Robert Burns, 1792

OLAUDAH EQUIANO

O laudah Equiano was born in the 1740s in what he described as a 'charming, fruitful vale' named Essaka in what is now southeastern Nigeria. His father was a chief; his people lived peacefully, several days travel from the ocean. But one day, when his parents were working in the fields, a gang jumped over the walls of their house and grabbed Olaudah and his sister. Six months later he was on a slave ship.

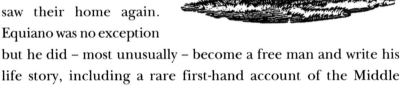

Few African slaves ever saw their home again. Equiano was no exception but he did – most unusually – become a free man and write his life story, including a rare first-hand account of the Middle Passage aboard the slave ship:

> *The stench of the hold ... now that the whole ship's cargo were*
> *confined together ... became absolutely pestilential ... so crowded*
> *that each had scarcely room to turn himself ... This wretched*
> *situation was aggravated by the galling of the chains, now become*
> *insupportable, and the filth of the necessary tubs [latrine buckets],*
> *into which the children often fell, and were almost suffocated. The*
> *shrieks of the women, and the groans of the dying, rendered the*
> *whole a scene of horror almost inconceivable.*

Sometimes slaves tried to kill themselves by jumping overboard. The sailors would race to retrieve them before the sharks could feast. Most of the time, male slaves were bound by chains, manacles, neck rings and padlocks. Laid like spoons, they were unable to lie full length nor stand upright, and were caked in faeces and urine. Women slaves were kept separate, enabling easier access for the crew.

Equiano's boat reached Bridgetown, Barbados – then possibly the busiest port in the Americas and home to the sugar trade, a business far crueller than the cotton fields in America. Sugar meant harder work, more disease and less food. Of the two million slaves shipped into the British West Indies for sugar, few lived long enough to breed. That compares poorly with the American South, where 400,000 slaves grew to a population of four million. The United States took 5–6% of African slaves shipped across the Atlantic; the majority of arrivals fed the sugar slaughterhouses of Brazil and the Caribbean. Cotton was hard, but sugar was hell.

Equiano was lucky. He avoided the sugar field and was sold to a naval officer, who took him around the world. He saw London and was probably the first African to see the Arctic. He learnt to read and wrote his life story. He met General Wolfe on the way to Quebec and encountered the young Horatio Nelson. But several times, just when he was feeling confident of his skills and position, he was sold again. However smart he may have been, white men could only see him as a slave.

Finally, Equiano got his freedom. In time he became known as one of the most famous faces – and voices – of the millions of Africans who were anonymous slaves.

The charity Survival works hard to protect the Guarani, Brazil's most numerous tribe. 500 years ago, the Guarani were one of the first peoples contacted by Europeans arriving in South America. Today, their 51,000 survivors still struggle to find land where they might live. They are threatened daily by violent ranchers. And like many generations before, they are vulnerable to being dragged into the hell of sugar plantations. Here's a recent report from Survival:

Brazil has one of the most highly-developed biofuels industries in the world. Sugar cane plantations were established in the 1980s and rely heavily on indigenous labour. Workers often work for pitiful wages under terrible conditions. In 2007, police raided a sugar cane alcohol distillery and discovered 800 Indians working and living in subhuman conditions. As many indigenous men are forced to seek work on the plantations, they are absent from their communities for long periods. This has a major impact on Guarani health and society. Sexually transmitted diseases and alcoholism have been introduced by returning workers and internal tensions and violence have increased. Over 80 new sugar cane plantations and alcohol distilleries are planned for the area of Mato Grosso do Sul – many of which are to be built on ancestral land claimed by the Guarani.

WILLIAM HOLLANDER

Here's a song about a slaver, and a pirate to boot. He's not a rich captain, just an Irish lad who leaves home for excitement, then makes a series of bad decisions. The first written record of this song dates from the late 19th century, but it might have been sung in different versions as far back as the 1700s. [There are more details of this and all the book's songs in the Index of Songs at the back]. Tales of piracy are often rakish or romantic. Not here. Add in clear-eyed detail about slavery and you have a first-rate confessional ballad.

The Flying Cloud

My name is William Hollander as you may understand,
I was born in the town of Waterford in Erin's happy land.
I being young and in my prime, kind fortune on me smiled,
My parents doted upon me, I was their only child.

My father bound me to a trade in Waterford's town,
He bound me to a cooper there in the name of William Brown.
I served my master faithfully for eighteen months and more,
Till I slipped on board The Ocean Queen bound for Bermuda's shore.

After some time sailing we arrived at Bermuda's shore.
Lying in harbour there I met in wi' Captain More,
He asked me if I'd ship with him, a slavish voyage to go,
To the burning shores of Africa, where the coffee seed do grow.

The Flying Cloud like a gallant ship carrying 600 tons and more,
She could outsail any clipper ship hailing out of Baltimore,

With her canvas white as the driven snow and on it there's no specks,
And forty men and fourteen guns she carried below her decks.

After some time sailing we arrived at the African shores,
Till five hundred of those poor souls from their native land we tore.
The crew they marched them on the deck and stowed them down below,
Scarce eighteen inches to each man was all they had to go.

So we set sail the very next day with our cargo of slaves
But better far for these poor souls they had been in their graves
For the fever and the plague set in which carried them half away
We dragged their bodies on the deck and heaved them in the sea.

After some time sailing we arrived at the Cuba shore.
We sold them to the planters there to be slaves for evermore,
The cotton and the rice to hoe beneath the burning sun,
To lead a hard and wretched life till their career was run.

After our money being all spent we set out to the seas again,
The captain stood upon the deck and spoke unto us men,
He said there's gold and silver to be had if we with him remained,
We'd hoist aloft a pirate flag and scour the Spanish Main.

We all agreed except five young lads so they were told to land.
Two of them were Boston boys and two from Newfoundland,
The other was an Irish boy belonging to Tramore,
I wish if I had joined these lads and gone with them on shore.

We sank and plundered many a ship down on the Spanish Main,
Leaving many a widow and orphan in sorrow to remain.
To the crews we gave no quarter but gave them watery graves,
For the saying of our captain was: 'Dead men will tell no tales.'

We ran and fought with many a ship, both frigates and liners too,
Till, at last, a British man-o-war, The Dunmow, hove in view,
She fired a shot across our bows as we ran before the wind,
And a chainshot cut our mainmast down and we fell far behind.

They beat our crew to quarters as they drew up alongside,
And soon across our quarter-deck there ran a crimson tide,
We fought until they killed our captain and twenty of our men,
Then a bombshell set our ship on fire, we had to surrender then.

It's now to Newgate we have come, bound down with iron chains,
For the sinking and the plundering of ships on the Spanish Main,
The judge he found us guilty, we were condemned to die.
Young men a warning by me take, lead not such a life as I.

So it's fare you well, old Waterford and the girl I do adore,
I'll never kiss your cheek again, I'll squeeze your hand no more,
Oh whiskey and bad company first made a wretch of me,
Oh young men, a warning by me take and shun all piracy.

SLAVERY AND SONG

Amazing grace! How sweet the sound
That saved a wretch like me!
I once was lost, but now am found;
Was blind, but now I see.

This most loved of American hymns was published, famously, by an ex-slaver who had seen the light. But he'd also heard the slaves. It's possible that the captain-turned-preacher John Newton based his abolitionist apology on a song sung by the cargo he'd carried; there's a sway to the rhythm of *Amazing Grace* that hints at an African song for accompanying labour. If so, it would be fitting provenance for this call for deliverance; even if, as ever, it enabled a white man to profit from the black man's pain.

Few slave songs survive. There are spirituals from later times – and there are many, many songs deriving rhythm or tone from African music – but few authentic expressions of the slaves themselves. One reason for this is that slaves didn't want to sing them. As the freed American slave Frederick Douglass wrote:

> *I have been utterly astonished, since I came to the north, to find*
> *persons who could speak of the singing among slaves as evidence*
> *of their contentment and happiness. It is impossible to conceive*
> *of a greater mistake. Slaves sing most when they are most*
> *unhappy. The songs of the slave represent the sorrows of his*
> *heart; and he is relieved by them, only as an aching heart is*
> *relieved by its tears.*

In 1790 a select committee of the British House of Commons examining slavery heard from an eye-witness:

> *After meals they are made to jump in their irons [up on the*
> *deck]. This is called dancing by the slave-dealers. In every ship*

he [the witness] has been desired to flog such as would not jump.
He had generally a cat of nine tails in his hand ... in his ship
even those who had the flux, scurvy and such edematous
swellings in their legs as made it painful to them to move at all,
were compelled to dance by the cat ... the captain ordered them to
sing, and they sung songs of sorrow.

Yet the singing of slaves had a huge effect upon maritime music. Ships have always been tuneful places: there are work songs of Egyptian fishermen going back to 2500 BC; singing helps ease the labour of hauling ropes, furling sails and turning capstans.

The best-known working songs of the sea are shanties: vigorous, repetitive chants that arose most noticeably upon merchant vessels of the 19th century. On the surface, slavery had little effect on shanties. Britain outlawed the trade in 1807, the US 1808, long before we hear of shantying. But some argue slavery's main impact on sea song was the arrival of black singing and black sailors. Call-and-response – the heart of shanty – was central to African music. It lent itself to repetitive labour. Where traditional western songs had a beginning, middle and end, African call-and-response singing would last as long as the task in hand. And it invited improvisation: to have fun, to comment on what was going on, to lighten the task. It was perfect for work on board.

Of course shanties had other sources: fishing and rowing songs from the Pacific, English folk songs, Celtic fiddle tunes, even Russian work songs such as that of the Volga Boatmen. We have Elizabethan hauling songs from the 1500s.

But many shanty experts see the influence of Africa as crucial. The call-and-response came from African farm songs – it later went into spirituals, gospel music and the blues. There were also field hollers, shouts and moans, which slaves would use to communicate secretly with each other, strange language that emerged in the shanties. And just as the English banned the bagpipe after the Jacobite Revolt, so they banned African slaves from using drums. This prompted slaves to use vocal sounds to create percussion; hence again some of the noises and rhythms of shanties.

Africa also provided many shantymen. These were the soloists who led the song, standing beside the working sailors and providing the calls for as long as the work demanded. They had strong voices and sharp minds to keep the crew amused. The Irish were often reckoned the best white singers, but many felt the finest shantymen were of African origin. They couldn't sing like this unless they were free men, and it took some time into the 19th century before a free black man felt safe enough to sign aboard a ship without danger of being enslaved once again.

Here is a shanty from the Sea Islands off Georgia which, unusually, appears to be the voice of a slave and, even more unusually, talks fondly of a slave driver called Riley, who was presumably kinder than most.

Goodbye My Riley-O

Riley, Riley, where are you?
Oh, Riley, oh man!
Riley, Riley, where are you?
Bye, bye, my Riley, oh man!

Riley's gone to London Bay,
Oh, Riley, oh man!
London Bay so far away,
Bye, bye, my Riley, oh man!

Riley's gone to Liverpool,
Oh, Riley, oh man!
Riley's gone an' I'll go too,
Bye, bye, my Riley, oh man!

Wish I was Captain Riley's son,
Oh, Riley, oh man!
I'd stay at home an' drink good rum,
Bye, bye, my Riley, oh man!

I thought I heard the Captain say,
Oh, Riley, oh man!
Tomorrow be our sailing day,
Bye, bye, my Riley, oh man!

Riley, Riley, where are you?
Oh, Riley, oh man!
Riley, Riley, where are you?
Bye, bye, my Riley, oh man!

There's an element of music hall about this next broadside ballad. Hiss those nasty slavers! Attend that plaintive mother! And noble England, rescue the poor Negro slave! Dated probably from around 1800, this cheaply-printed sheet – with two songs per broadside – might have been glued to a tavern wall for easy reference when sung in chorus.

The Slave Ship Ballad

The first grey dawn of the morning was beaming,
The bright rays shone forth, the glad spirit of light,
The rising sun over the ocean was streaming,
And dispell'd with his rays the dark shadows of night,
The air – oh, how pure! – and the morning was mild,
And the waters lay hushed like a sleeping child.
What cheer? cried the mate, as he passed to and fro,
What cheer? Art thou watching? Is all right below?
All's right! cried a voice, the hatches are tight –
As the chains that are binding the slaves this night.

Up, up, with the anchor, then let us away,
Spread the sails, 'tis a favouring wind,
And long 'ere the break of the morning we'll leave
The coast of old Africa behind.

The moonlight will follow our track o'er the deep
As we start through the sparkling wave,
For our cargo of beings are all hushed in sleep,
As though they were hushed in the grave
Then up with the anchor and let us away
We dare not – we must not, no longer delay!

Softly, softly let us away,
Softly, softly let us away.

Gloomily stood the
captain, with his arms
upon his breast,
With his cold brow sternly
knitted, and iron lip
compressed.
Are all well whipp'd below
there? Aye, aye! the
seamen said,
Heave up the worthless
lubbers, the dying and
the dead.

Help! Oh help! thou God of Christians, save a mother from despair.
Cruel white man sold my children – Oh! God of Mercy hear my prayer,
I'm young, and strong, and hearty – he's a sick and feeble boy:
Take me, whip me, chain me, starve me, Oh, God! in mercy, save my boy.
They've kill'd my child, they've killed my child, the mother shriek'd
– now all is o'er –
Down the savage captain struck her, lifeless, on the vessel's floor.

Old England, sweet land of the brave and the free
Whose home is the waters, whose flag sweeps the sea!
O stretch forth thy hand, o'er the ocean's dark waves,
Protecting the poor and unfortunate slaves!
And nations that boast they are free shall repent,
For thousands of souls to Eternity sent;
He that forwards the cause, on the verge of the grave,
Shall be blest with a prayer, from the poor Negro Slave!

THE TROUBLE WITH TEA

S ugar drew slavers west, but tea pulled them east. As the tea trade grew between China and Europe from the late 18th century, so it spawned fresh channels of mass slavery. Many coolies went to work the fields of Fujian Province, home of the Chinese tea so loved by the English. But slaves were also needed to source goods that could be traded for tea. It was handy that some items most prized by the Chinese – birds' nests, mother of pearl and sea cucumber – could be harvested nearby in the South China Sea. And so arose a vicious local slaving industry.

Based around the Sulu archipelago between Borneo and the Philippines, this enslaved unwitting coastal villagers throughout Southeast Asia, then forced them back to work in fisheries or birds' nest caves. The colonial authorities decried such barbaric piracy, of course, and Sulu slavers took special pleasure in enslaving vulnerable, white Europeans who crossed their path. But trade was the prevailing reality. This slavery prospered from the West's thirst for tea, and survived through the close links between slavers and traders, and collusion between pirates and local rulers. And, as we shall later see, such a pattern persists to this day, whereby Western demand for prawns drives the enslavement of Cambodians to work on Thai fishing boats.

Two centuries ago, the 'people fishers' relied on vessels called *prahus* – heavily armed and rowed by slaves – to hunt the thousands of small islands that fill the region. Built like floating castles to process and protect the catch, these ship were often too big to do the actual angling. For that, they would send out raiding canoes before dawn, a few pirates disguised as fishermen with many more lying down out of sight. Quiet and quick, they'd pick off people fishing or gathering mussels. Children were a profitable haul, and might also bring mothers who could not bear separation. Swift violence awaited any who resisted. The canoes would vanish before villages could muster their defence.

Back on board, the first task was to turn the captives into slaves. Just as the African slavers had learnt, resistance was most likely in the early days after capture, while mental and physical strength remained high. The trick, therefore, was to weaken the captives' bodies and resolve. Near starvation served both these ends, while beatings and summary executions bred the hopelessness that spurs acceptance.

Stronger captives would be tied up for months, their limbs thrashed with bamboo so they could not swim or run away. A Dutch captain C. Z. Pieters described his 1838 capture by slavers in the Celebes Sea. Late one evening, ten *prahus* attacked his cutter *Petronella*. Badly wounded, he passed out:

> *When I came again to my senses, I found that I was stripped naked and bound in a prahu ... tied up by the hands, feet and neck. The rope at which captives are tied by the neck is taken off in the day-time. At six o'clock in the evening, whether they are inclined to sleep or not, they must lie down and are bound by the feet, hands and neck to the deck of the prahu.*

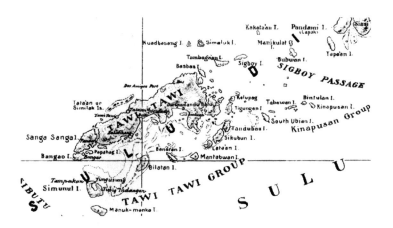

Walking Liverpool's dockside in the late 1840s, you might have met a mute, shattered man, proffering a cheap handbill. His name was William Edwards and his sad note read:

TO A GENEROUS PUBLIC

I am a poor young man who have had the misfortune of having my Tongue cut out of my mouth on my passage home from the Coast of China, to Liverpool, in 1845, by the Malay Pirates, on the Coast of Malacca. There were Fourteen of our Crew taken prisoners and kept on shore four months; some of whom had their eyes put out, some their legs cut off, for myself I had my Tongue cut out. We were taken about 120 miles to sea; we were then given a raft and let go, and were three days and three nights on the raft, and ten out of fourteen were lost. We were picked up by the ship James, bound to Boston, in America, and after our arrival we were sent home to Liverpool, in the ship Sarah James ... I am now obliged to appeal to a Generous Public for support, and any small donation you please to give will be thankfully received by

Your obedient servant, WILLIAM EDWARDS

It's a shame the memories of a few westerners have survived better than those of hundreds of thousands of Indonesians, Malaysians and Filipinos. Today, though, we are better able to put a name, and a face, to slaves from Asia.

For example, Suey San from Cambodia. In 2012, unable to support his family as a builder, he left for the rich prospects of neighbouring Thailand. But soon finding himself exploited on a Bangkok building site, he decided to go home. He turned himself in at a police station, hoping to be deported as an illegal immigrant. But the 'police' handed him to some slavers, who sold him onto a fishing boat, where he was forced to work 20 hours a day pulling nets and gutting fish. They gave him amphetamines for energy and threw overboard those too weak to work. Many such slave ships spend years at sea, trading slaves from one boat to another. Recently the multinational Nestlé admitted that fish caught in this way supplied their pet food.

In 2014 Ei Ei Lwin also made the mistake of talking to Thai police. A Burmese migrant, he was stopped at the port of Songkhla by police demanding a bribe, which he could not afford. They sold him to a broker, who sent him to work on a trawler, where he claimed to witness a score of people killed in front of him. Boat owners today are reckoned to pay as little as £250 per slave to the brokers; they then deduct that fee from the slave in the form of labour.

£250 for a life. One anti-trafficking activist claims such modern slaves cost 95% less than they did at the height of the 19th century slave trade. No longer are such humans viewed as investments, but as disposable commodities.

And who is driving demand for this slavery? If you buy prawns from the supermarket, it might be you. Many food retailers from Europe, America and Australia source cheap product from Thai companies like Charoen Pokphand, which buy from the boat captains and the shrimp factories. At factories in places such as Samut Sakhon, Burmese labourers spend 16 hours a day with their hands in ice water, gutting and shelling prawns; where Khine Zin Soe, 24, was forced to keep working even after she miscarried and bled for four days, or where Win Win Than, 25, was handcuffed while pregnant for trying to run away.

Little changes in global trade. Where a worker in 1800 sat down for a cup of tea, or today we grab a prawn sandwich for lunch, our innocent acts can trigger a chain of cruelty that spurs slavery somewhere else in the world.

The *Flashman* books by George MacDonald Fraser are not an obvious resource for a study of slavery; their unreconstructed jingoism sits awkwardly beside modern analysis. But, dammit, they often emit an unparalleled whiff of authenticity. Here's a passage from *Flashman's Lady*, where he describes a nasty armada gathering in Kuching. Though fictional, it well portrays the links between pirates, local rulers, colonial traders and the Royal Navy back in the 19th century.

I remember the long war-praus with their steep sheers and forests of oars, being warped one after another into the jetty by sweating, squealing Malay steersmen, and the Raja's native allies pouring aboard – a chattering, half-naked horde of Dyaks, some in kilts and sarongs, others in loin-cloths and leggings, some in turbans, some with feathers in their hair, but all grinning and ugly as sin, loaded with their vile sumpitan-pipes and arrows, their kreeses and spears, all fit to frighten the French.

Then there were the Malay swordsmen who filled the sampans – big, flat-faced villains with muskets and the terrible, straight-bladed kampilan cleavers in their belts; the British tars in their canvas smocks and trousers and straw hats, their red faces grinning and sweating while they loaded Dido's pinnace, singing 'Whisky, Johnny' as they stamped and hauled; the silent Chinese cannoneers whose task it was to lash down the small guns in the bows of the sampans and longboats, and stow the powder kegs and matches; the slim, olive-skinned Linga pirates who manned Paitingi's spy-boats – astonishing craft these, for all the world like Varsity racing-shells, slim frail needles with thirty paddles that could skim across the water as fast as a man can run. They darted among the other vessels – the long, stately praus, the Dido's pinnace, the cutters and launches and canoes, the long sloop Jolly Bachelor which was Brooke's own flagship;

*and the flower of our fleet, the East India paddle-steamer
Phlegethon, with her massive wheel and platform, and her
funnel belching smoke. They all packed the river, in
a great tangle of oars and cordage and rubbish,
and over it rang the constant chorus of curses and
commands in half a dozen languages; it looked
like a waterman's picnic gone mad.*

BLACKBIRDING

In July 1883 a Pacific islander called Bakala left his home in Vanuatu to go fishing. Walking along the beach at sunrise, he saw a ship a short distance away. 'She had two boats, painted red, trying to get men; the ship had been anchored there for two nights,' he later reported. The two red boats slowly rowed toward Bakala, each propelled by the oars of four sailors from a nearby island. As was typical of kidnappers in the western Pacific, one boat landed on the beach while the other stayed close to shore to help in case of trouble.

One of the sailors called out to Bakala, 'Come here, you.' He answered, 'I do not know your ship.' 'Come near to the boat and let us have a talk,' countered the sailor, whose name was Sam. As Bakala walked closer, he was seized by Sam, who dragged him into the boat, which rowed out to sea before fellow villagers could come to his aid. As Bakala remembered, 'the men were all armed with guns; when Sam pulled me into the boat I called out, and cried "Do not steal me, Sam, put me ashore again."' But Bakala was hauled on board the ship, the fifty-ton schooner *Caledonia* from Noumea in the French colony of New Caledonia. The white master ignored Bakala's pleas for release. Bakala got talking with another prisoner called Usi from the Solomon Islands who'd previously been working under indenture in Levuka, which had been the capital of Fiji's cotton boom. Soon afterwards Bakala and Usi were set to work on a plantation.

When the US Civil War shattered cotton production in North America, replacement plantations sprung up across the western Pacific. Their labour was supplied in similar practice to that of the American South: European slave ships used local slave masters to 'recruit' poor Melano-Polynesians. This became known as blackbirding. The bulk of these 'labourers' were taken to

Australia and Fiji, where the British Colonial Office turned a blind eye to practices long banned elsewhere in the empire. Even so, cries from abolitionists grew stronger and a Royal Navy commander called George Palmer, who'd led anti-slave patrols in West Africa, went to investigate in 1869. He found an English schooner called the *Daphne:*

> *fitted up precisely like an African slaver, minus the irons, with 100 natives on board, who had been brought here from the New Hebrides ... they were stark naked and had not even a mat to lie upon; the shelves were just the same as might be knocked up for a lot of pigs, no bunks or partitions of any sort being fitted, and yet the vessel was inspected by a government officer of Queensland.*

Though Palmer set the slaves free, the Queensland courts overturned his ruling and allowed the *Daphne* to continue its trade. In the decades after 1863 Australia imported over 60,000 such 'migrant labourers'. [It kicked most of them out between 1906-1908 under the White Australia policy.] Many Melano-Polynesians also worked outside the British colonies, in California and Chile or as Pacific sailors. They were known as *kanakas*, taken from the Hawaiian word for man. This led to one of the most famous shanties of all:

> *I heard, I heard the old man say*
> > *John Kanaka-naka too-lai-e*
> *Today, today is a holiday*
> > *John Kanaka-naka too-ley-ay*
> *Too-ley-ay, ooh! Too-ley-ay!*
> > *John Kanaka-naka too-ley-ay*

MUTINY

O h, those irrepressible entrepreneurs. Several decades after selling slaves was banned in Britain, a new triangular trade arose to serve sugar interests. This covered greater distance, connecting Europe, China and the Americas, but – as before – the middle passage carried slaves for the labour-hungry plantations of the Caribbean. The trade started in Europe or the United States, where ships stuffed with steel and textiles set off for China. There they took on coolies – indentured Chinese labourers – whom they brought back and sold in Cuba or nearby, where they loaded up with sugar and honey for their home ports.

The authorities pretended this was not slavery because the coolies were indentured for fixed term, after which they were free. But like white indentured servants in the 18th century, few survived their term. As with slavery, this business was lucrative for traders, handy for the authorities and brutal for migrants.

And, as with slavery, it was no secret. In June 1864 *Harper's New Monthly Magazine* gave its New York readers a first-hand account of conditions on board a coolie trader called the *Norway*. Its writer

Edgar Holden was an American physician who, as a passenger, was witness to some remarkable events. He described the measures taken to secure crew and paying passengers against the human cargo below:

> *Over every hatchway save one were set iron gratings to prevent too free access from below to the upper deck ... the gratings were made of bars of iron, arched in the centre, and having a circular opening of eight or nine inches diameter at the summit of the arch ... on the spar deck a barricade was built, running athwart ship ... twelve feet wide, two feet high, and arranged so that a guard of armed men could, from their station, command the whole deck.*

Mutiny was a daily risk on ships like the *Norway*, where a small crew had to sail and guard itself against more than 1,000 slaves, desperate and poorly treated. Three days after loading its cargo in Macao, the ship faced its first bloody dispute as one captive attacked another with a stolen cleaver. Shortly thereafter, 'a bright gleam of flame shot up from the forecastle and a yell like that of ten thousand demons burst on the still night'.

Sailors locked the main hatch and armed themselves with 'every blunderbuss, cutlass and pistol ... several of the foremost rioters were striving to force the door with cleavers stolen from the cooks, and had partially succeeded in prying it open against a dozen men who were endeavouring to fasten a spar across outside'. The struggle became touch-and-go, with the slaves threatening to burn their way to freedom. Sailors threw tarpaulins over the forward hatches and poured water into the hold to douse the flames. This caused such smoke that the captives crowded upwards to get air. 'But men, stationed at every loop-hole and crevice, shot down with remorseless vengeance every one of them who appeared within range, till ere long not one could be seen from any point on deck.' 70 died in the mutiny. By the time the *Norway* reached Havana four months later, a further 60 had died – and 60 more were killed by dysentery while in harbour. Such a mortality rate was not unusual on coolie ships, and matched that of slavery and early convict transportation.

Mutiny persists wherever desperate people are contained by unscrupulous traffickers. Here is a news report from 23rd July 2014:

> *Italian police have arrested five men on suspicion of murdering and throwing overboard more than 100 fellow migrants on a treacherous crossing from Tunisia. Survivors told police how a life-or-death fight broke out when those who were riding in the hold of the boat, suffocating from heat and lack of oxygen, desperately tried to find room on the packed deck. To keep the migrants below the deck, the five men indiscriminately stabbed and assaulted the migrants before throwing them overboard, according to police. Twenty-nine bodies, including a baby, were later recovered from the hold of what had been a badly overcrowded fishing boat. A further 110 people are believed to have been thrown into the ocean by their fellow passengers on the horror crossing from Tunisia. According to some of the migrants, they paid people smugglers $1,000–$2,000 for a place on deck and $200–$500 for one in the hold. The excessive heat and fumes from the motor drove those in the hold to try to get out. When they were pushed back and the ladder to the deck was removed and the portal closed, the migrants in the hold mutinied, police said. 'In a matter of minutes the heat became unbearable and the air was unbreathable due to the fumes from the motor,' a police statement said. 'Desperation drove the prisoners to force open the door and climb onto deck where the tragedy occurred.'*

I am a Poor Wayfaring Stranger

Sung widely within both black and white communities in
19th century America, and proudly sporting the gospel
cloak of journey and suffering, this song draws deep on the
experience of involuntary export.

I am a poor wayfaring stranger
A-trav'ling through this land of woe.
And there's no sickness, toil or danger
In that bright world to which I go.
I'm going home to see my father
I'm going there no more to roam;
I'm just a-going over Jordan
I'm just a-going over home.

I know dark clouds will gather 'round me
I know my way is steep and rough;
But beauteous fields lie just beyond me
Where souls redeemed their vigil keep.
I'm going there to meet my mother
She said she'd meet me when I come
I'm just a-going over Jordan
I'm just a-going over home.

I want to wear a crown of glory
When I get home to that bright land
I want to shout Salvation's story
In concert with that bloodwashed band.
I'm going there to meet my Saviour
To sing His praises forevermore
I'm only going over Jordan
I'm only going over home.

THE BRITISH APPETITE FOR ABOLITION

By modern standards, no place on earth was particularly humane in the late 18th century. In Britain, most people's lives remained nasty, brutish and relatively short. Yet by the 1790s more than 300,000 Britons were refusing to eat slave-grown sugar, and their reasons for this were mostly compassionate. The early Abolitionists quickly learnt the power of petitions in mobilising public outrage.

But why were Britons keener on abolishing the slave trade than, say, Americans – who otherwise rather liked their independence? Distance played a part. As Adam Hochschild points out in *Bury the Chains; the British Struggle to Abolish Slavery*, 'Britain's slaves weren't in Britain. To push for ending slavery was to threaten planters and ship owners, but it did not, as in the United States, risk secession or civil war. And with the slaves on the other side of the ocean, for Britons to oppose slavery did not threaten their own way of life. Slaves were not cooking the meals or doing the laundry or working the fields in Britain itself.'

But that was also true in France and Spain, and in countries far more literate than Britain, such as Sweden or Holland – yet in none of these places was Abolition so popular. What was the difference in Britain?

Here's a clue. Let's return to Olaudah Equiano, the African slave who wrote his life story. As the slave of a naval officer, Equiano spent years with the Royal Navy, and during this time he got to work in a press gang. There's an irony – a captive black man putting white men in chains.

Britain controlled the oceans because it had the largest fleet. During the Napoleonic wars the Royal Navy had 1,000 ships and more than 140,000 men afloat. Up to half of all seamen during wartime were 'pressed', meaning seized for service. The press gangs took anyone they could. A man might be down the pub, tending his garden, or getting married, and three hours later find himself chained upon a frigate bound for the Indian Ocean, facing years of flogging and maggots. Men in seaports, London too, lived in fear of the press. And some fought back. During the American Revolution, when 80,000 Englishmen were pressed, riots broke out in at least 22 British seaports. That may be why the British were so sensitive to violent enslavement.

A strong navy enabled Britain to escape the weaknesses of, say, the Dutch empire, whose isolated colonies lacked a reliable lifeline to the motherland. Naval blockade helped contain Napoleon and his far stronger armies. All this depended on the press gang. So, to an extent, did those fighting tyranny in the world: in 1776 Jefferson listed impressment as one of George III's crimes in the Declaration of Independence.

In Britain it was harder to decry the press gang publicly, so revulsion for violent enslavement was channelled into opposing the slave trade. Many leading abolitionists had direct experience of the press. As Hochschild explains: 'Olaudah Equiano, as a sailor, took part in it. John Newton was a victim of it. John Clarkson, as a naval officer, was intimately familiar with it. Granville Sharp denounced it as heatedly as he did slavery.'

The press gang was radically different from conscription. It represented kidnapping by armed men – and this particularly British method of officially oppressing the public had a significant effect upon the progress of liberty worldwide.

The Press Gang

As I walked out on London Street
A press gang there I chanced to meet
They asked me if I'd join the fleet
  On board of a man-o'-war, boys

Come brother shipmates tell me true
What kind of treatment they give you
That I may know before I go
  On board of a man-o'-war, boys

When I got there to my surprise
I found they'd told me shocking lies
There was a row and a jolly old row
  On board of a man-o'-war, boys

The first thing they done they took me in hand
They lashed me with a tarred strand
They flogged me till I could not stand
  On board of a man-o'-war, boys

They hung me up by my two thumbs
They left me til the blood did run
They cut me down, I hit the ground
  On board of a man-o'-war, boys

When next I get my foot on shore
To see them London girls once more
I'll never go to sea no more
  On board of a man-o'-war, boys

THE LIFE AND SUFFERINGS OF JAMES M'LEAN, AN IMPRESSED AMERICAN CITIZEN & SEAMAN

A merican sailors were easy prey for the Royal Navy, which claimed they were British deserters and pressed them accordingly. One such victim, James M'Lean from Hartford, Connecticut, endured 17 years in service during the Napoleonic wars. Despite sailing all around the world, and jumping ship several times, he could not escape the all powerful Navy. His account of his travails starts on 10th March 1798 as a crewman aboard the *Glory-Ann* of Philadelphia, just leaving Grenada:

> *We had no sooner let go our anchor, than an English Man of War's boat came on board and pressed me and two more of the Seamen, and carried us on board the Madrass, 50 gun ship, commanded by John Dilks, who asked me for my protection. I shewed him one from a Notary Public in New York, by the name of Keyes; he replied, 'I could get one, if I was in America, for half a crown, as good as that.' He further said, 'it is of no use for you to pretend that you are an American, for you was born in Scotland.' The first Lieutenant then stepped up and said, 'yes, that he was, for I knew his friends in Greenock.' The Capt made answer, 'he shall then do his duty in the main-top.' The day following I went to the Capt and told him, I hoped he would send me aboard of my own ship, as I was an American citizen; to which he replied, 'You Scotch Rascal, if you do not go to your duty, I'll punish you.'*

Soon M'Lean found himself fighting for Nelson at the Battle of the Nile. Later at Torbay he attempted his first escape, joining an English fishing boat to London then an American schooner bound for Boston. Unfortunately a gale forced the latter into Falmouth where, sent ashore to gather water, he was pressed again, even more cruelly this time, for he was treated as a deserter. It was now 1801. M'Lean fought in several battles against the French, managed to send his parents a letter via an American frigate in Gibraltar, and returned to Portsmouth in 1803 expecting to be paid off. But again he was pressed, this time receiving 12 lashes and having two teeth knocked out when a lieutenant hit him with a speaking trumpet.

In April 1805 M'Lean escaped again in Plymouth, hiding among a crowd of yard labourers. He signed on an English merchantman for Lisbon, then an American schooner for Brest, where he joined a French brig bound for Cayenne in the West Indies. But off Tenerife she was captured by an English frigate, whose captain again refused to believe he was an American, taking him in irons to St Helena to be hanged as a deserter. Instead, he was pressed again and saw more action in the Med, then, returning to England, he spent two months 'in a hulk' – a floating prison – while his ship was refitted. Reaching Bombay in May 1809 he set foot on land for the first time in three years. Thence he joined action against pirates in the Gulf of Persia, witnessing the massacre, by English marines, of 1,400 men, women and children in a town near Muscat.

After journeys to China, Macao, Bombay, St Helena, Hull and Gothenburg, M'Lean sailed in 1813 to Corunna in Spain on a supply ship for Wellington's army. Once again he did a runner. This time it worked. He made it to Lisbon, where the American consul gave him a passport and he boarded the *Zodiac*, a brig bound for the US. In November he arrived in Newport, Rhode Island – his first sight of American shore in more than 17 years:

> *Within three days I reached my father's house, and I leave it to*
> *you to judge of my feelings and their's on this interview. The*
> *sympathetic tear could not be suppressed; parental and filial*
> *affection were mutually interchanged, and every sentiment*
> *congenial to friends, was endeavoured to be reciprocated.*

Impressment makes a passing but crucial appearance in the 18th century ballad *The Bristol Bridegroom,* in which a mean Bristol merchant causes to be pressed the young carpenter with whom his daughter has fallen in love. But she is a valiant woman. She dresses up as a man and boards the same ship where, disguised as the surgeon's mate, she gets to save the life of her loved one. Many ballads told similar stories: of lovers cruelly separated, of bold women smuggling themselves aboard and of the perils of naval service. Though sung mainly for their love story, they packed in plenty of social comment.

The Bristol Bridegroom

You loyal lovers far and near, a true relation you shall hear,
Of a young couple who prov'd to be, a pattern of true loyalty.

A merchant did in Bristol dwell, as many people know full well;
He had a daughter of beauty bright, in whom he plac'd his heart's delight.

Yet notwithstanding all their love, a young carpenter did prove
To be the master of her heart; she often said, we'll never part.

Now when her father came to know his daughter loved a young man so,
He caus'd him to be prest to sea, to keep him from her company,

Which when his daughter came to hear, without the thought of dread or fear,
She drest herself in seaman's hue, and after him she did pursue.

Unto the Captain she did go, and said, right worthy sir, 'tis so,
You do want men, I understand, I'm free to fight with heart and hand.

The Captain straitway did reply, young man you're welcome heartily;
One guinea in her hand he gave, she passed for a seaman brave.

She then appeared for to be, a person of no mean degree;
With pretty fingers long and strait, she soon became the surgeon's mate.

It happened so that this same ship, a storming of the town of Dieppe,
She lay at anchor something nigh, where the cannon balls did fly.

Then the first man that wounded were, was this young bold ship carpenter:
When drums beat and trumpets sound, he in his breast receiv'd a wound.

She cur'd him in a little space, he often gaz'd upon her face;
Surgeon, said he, such eyes as thine, did formerly my heart entwine:

If ever I live to go on shore, and she be dead whom I adore,
I will thy true companion be, and ne'er forsake thy company.

Then without any more ado, into his arms she straitway flew,
And cries, My love, thou art my own, this have I done for thee alone.

Young lovers all a pattern take, when you a solemn contract make,
Stand to the same whate'er betide, as did this faithful loving bride.

CLEARANCE

L et's go north to the Scottish Highlands, right to the top, to Sutherland: the most isolated spot on the British mainland. And over to the Western Isles where most roads, even today, are single-tracked.

This is one of the great wildernesses of Europe, pretty and vacant. But it wasn't always so. Once many people lived in the Highlands and Islands, until they were forced out by a mix of poverty and one of history's less-known bouts of ethnic cleansing: the Highland Clearances.

Colonel Gordon of Cluny was a rich man, one of the richest in Scotland. His money came from farms in the east, in Aberdeenshire. In 1841 he heard of an opportunity: the laird of several Hebridean islands was bankrupt, which gave Gordon the chance to pick up a lot of land on the cheap. Yet the land in the west was not so fertile as the land in the east; it was no good for crops or beef. However, thought Gordon, it would be perfect for a new wonder product – the Great Cheviot sheep – ideal for squeezing profit from barren soil.

But there was a problem: the islands were full of people. These people were poor, and their long feudal servitude to clan chiefs had left them few resources, whether in money or spirit. That clan chief had now sold them to a businessman who cared little for old loyalties. Gordon viewed these wild, Gaelic-speaking peasants as aborigines – they must be cleared so the land could be grazed.

In July 1848 Gordon removed 150 residents from the island of Barra and put them on a boat to Glasgow. There he turned them onto the street, most penniless, few speaking any English. They'd thought they were going to Nova Scotia; instead, many ended up in the Glasgow night asylum. There were protests, but Gordon cared little. Year by year he cleared more people. In one season alone he removed 2,000 people from South Uist, Benbecula and Barra.

Colonel Gordon's clearances in the Western Isles caused public outrage. And how did he respond? He got crueller. In August 1851 he sent the *Admiral* transport to the port of Lochboisdale in South Uist. His factor Fleming took bands of armed officers to seize families and chase fugitives. They burnt the crofts, so those who hid in the hills could not rebuild easily. Carts loaded with bound men came over the sea from Benbecula at low tide. As observer Donald Macleod wrote:

> *Were you to see the racing and chasing of policemen, pursuing the outlawed natives, you would think you had been transported to the banks of the Gambia on the slave coast of Africa.*

Catherine Macphee of Iochdar in South Uist said, 'I have seen the big strong men, the champions of the country, the stalwarts of the world, being bound on Lochboisdale quay and cast into the ship as would be done to horses and cattle.'

Yet Colonel Gordon claimed every emigrant had volunteered to leave. This time he did fulfil his promise to get them over the Atlantic. But no more. The emigrants were dumped in Quebec, in late autumn, with no money, no warm clothing and the vicious winter just weeks away. The local medical officer was outraged:

I never saw a body of emigrants so destitute of clothing and bedding; many children of nine or ten had not a rag to cover them. One full-grown man passed my inspection with no other garment than a woman's petticoat.'

Why clothe animals? Nearly 50 years after slavery was banned, British communities were being cleared for grazing – and Gordon was just one of many landowners carrying out this barbarity. Worse still, it was becoming practice for landowners to clear communities not just for sheep, but simply because they could.

Knoydart is a mighty but melancholic estate on the Scottish mainland opposite the Isle of Skye. Its population, hit hard by the potato famine of the late 1840s, fell to only seventy families along the coast. Their position posed no threat to the Great Cheviot sheep, but their owner Mrs Macdonell wanted rid of a near-pauper population. In late August 1853 she arranged for the transport ship *Sillery* to anchor nearby. She sent men into the townships, armed with hammers and axes, to destroy the huts and force the residents onto the ship. Four hundred people were cleared. They were taken directly to Nova Scotia. Some claim, even today, that this was an act of charity: a landowner paying for the impoverished to travel from a place of no prospects to a land of plenty. And yes, the potato famine had exacerbated steady economic decline in the Highlands.

But landowners in Scotland held feudal attitudes far longer than their in England. They tended to view tenants as either chattels or squatters, and felt no need to humanise their dealings with them. In Knoydart, the residents were first told the *Sillery* would deport them to Australia, and they adjusted to that horrible prospect. But at the last moment, with no warning, their destination shifted to Canada.

John Prebble's great book on the Highland Clearances includes a translation of this Gaelic song, showing the scars of clearance:

A Dhomhnaill, a ghràidh mo chridhe

Oh Donald, love of my heart,
I am sorrowful, heavy and weary
in solitude, as I think
of all the misery that pursues me,
and of all my kinsmen lost to me.
It is not offended pride, not rage,
not a fierce and savage gloom,
not War even (that would be little),
but that Islay now has so few
of the youth that once were here.
They have been driven away
to America across the sea,
and there is no one left
with kindly feelings, or peace in him.

Prebble also quotes from the bard Kenneth Mackenzie, aka The Brahan Seer or the 'Scottish Nostradamus', some of whose mysterious lines from centuries before are taken to foretell the Highland Clearances:

I see the hills, the valley and the slopes,
But they do not lighten my sorrow.
I see the bands departing on the white-sailed ships.
I see the Gael rising from his door. I see the people going,
And there is no love for them in the north.

Clearance continues. Today the aborigines being cleared are often native tribes. The charity Survival, in its work to help such endangered communities, reported the murder of a Brazilian tribal leader after his people were cleared from their lands.

Marcos Veron was leader of the Guarani-Kaiowá community of Takuára in Brazil. For many years his people tried to recover a piece of their ancestral land after it was seized by a wealthy Brazilian, cleared of forest and turned into a vast cattle ranch. In April 1997, desperate after years of lobbying the government in vain, Marcos led his community back onto the ranch. They began to rebuild their houses and plant their own crops. But the rancher who had occupied the area went to court, and a judge ordered the Indians out. In October 2001, more than one hundred heavily armed police and soldiers forced the Indians to leave their land once again. They ended up living under plastic sheets by the side of a highway. While still in Takuára, Marcos said, 'This here is my life, my soul. If you take me away from this land, you take my life.' His words came tragically true in 2003, when, during another attempt to return peacefully to his land, he was viciously beaten to death by employees of the rancher.

THE SLAVES SPEAK GAELIC

C ape Fear is hot, dank and flat. This coastal plain in North Carolina must have felt strange to the Scottish emigrants arriving there in the mid 18th century, even despite its deep forest of pine. But the land was cheap and it was fertile. Soon Cape Fear started filling with settlements. To work the land, there were poor Highlanders – many freshly cleared from Western Scotland – and there were African slaves.

Nearby in Georgia the first Scottish settlers had resisted slavery, on good Presbyterian principle. Some ministers, mainly Ulster Scots covenanters, moved their communities west to states less infested with slavery. But in North Carolina men such as

Farquhard Campbell and Archibald MacNeil bought slaves enthusiastically. Those cleared as aborigines from their own land often treated even more cruelly the aborigines they encountered in new lands. People prove capable, time after time, of passing on the misery they've received themselves, and adding some extra 'just for you'.

Cape Fear particularly drew settlers from the Western Highlands and Skye. Flora MacDonald of South Uist, who helped Bonnie Prince Charlie to escape the Hanoverian soldiers after the failed revolt of 1745, later landed in Wilmington and settled nearby in North Carolina. She may have known a lovely Gaelic lullaby about exile that's set in the Carolinas. As Billy Kay introduces this song in *The Scottish World: A Journey Into the Scottish Diaspora*, 'It was once said that America was built on a lie, because mothers sent their children to sleep reassuring them that there were no wild animals or hostile Indians outside the cabin door who were determined to come and get them. The homesickness and sense of loss felt by the bard who composed this song, however, overwhelms any desire to soften the reality for the dovering bairn:'

Dean Cadalan Samhach

Gur h-ann an Amerigeadh tha sinn an dràst
Fo dhubhar na coille nach teirig gu bràth
...
Ann an àite leam fhèin far nach
Èistear mr brhòn;
Madaidh-allaidh ag èigheach
Is bèistean ro mhòr
Ann an dùthaich nan Reubal far na
thrèig sinn Righ Deòrs

We are now in America
at the edge of the never-ending forest

...

All alone in this place where my grief
cannot be heard;
Wolves and giant beasts howling
in the land of Rebels where we have
forsaken King George

Slaves often took the name, language and culture of their master. So in Cape Fear there were many Gaelic-speaking African slaves. One ad for a runaway black slave in the mid 1700s read: 'He will be easy to identify, for he only speaks Gaelic.' Some black churches continued to pray in Gaelic even after abolition. An African fiddler called John 'Jack' McGeachy was known for his mastery of Highland music. Trumpeter Dizzy Gillespie talked of the influence of Scottish culture on black music (note his Scottish surname, like that of Louis Armstrong or Charlie Mingus/ Menzies). Some claim that the Highland church practice of 'precenting the line' – whereby a precentor sings the first line of a psalm for the congregation to follow – helped inspire the 'lining out' of black church music.

One should be wary of overstating such observations, especially from those seeking to justify slavery with the 'well it wasn't all bad' argument. But the determination of Highlanders to rebuild Gaelic culture brought some odd anomalies to the cultural broth of the Americas.

LE GRAND DÉRANGEMENT

In the mid 18th century, Britain fought France for control of Nova Scotia, New Brunswick and Prince Edward Island in what is now Canada. Britain won. It promptly deported the local French-speaking population, who were known as Acadians. Around 11,500 Acadians, 80 per cent of their total, were sent to Britain's American colonies or to France. Many went on to Louisiana, creating its French-speaking Cajun community. But many, as with all deportations, died in transit.

On 20th October 1758 the British transport *Duke William* left Ile St Jean on Prince Edward Island with 360 Acadian prisoners. It formed part of a fateful fleet, crossing to France at the wrong time of year. Its sister ship *Ruby* ran aground in the Azores, drowning 213 deportees. Then the *Violet*, another of the convoy, sank with 218 Acadians aboard. While watching this, powerless to help, the *Duke William* sprung a leak. Captives and crew together pumped desperately for three days. Captain Nichols wrote, 'We continued in this dismal situation three days; the ship, notwithstanding our endeavours, full of water, and expected to sink every minute.' But the ship by now lay close to the English Channel, so there was hope of rescue from a passing vessel. Nichols co-ordinated the pumping with the Acadian priest Girard and the community elder Noel Doiron.

On the morning of 13th December they spotted two English vessels. 'The old man [Doiron] took me in his aged arms, and cried for joy,' wrote Nichols. But the two ships ignored them. Then a Danish ship appeared. Again they thought they might be saved but, again, their pleas were ignored. The *Duke William* was now close to sinking. It had no lifeboats, just three small boats which might carry a handful of those aboard. Doiron consulted with the Acadians, which included his wife and over 120 members of his extended family. As the captain later wrote:

About half an hour after, the old gentleman came to me, crying; he took me in his arms, and said he came with the voice of the whole people, to desire that I and my men would endeavour to save our lives, in our boats; and as they could not carry them, they would on no consideration be the means of drowning us. They were well convinced, by all our behaviour, that we had done everything in our power for their preservation, but that God Almighty had ordained them to be drowned, and they hoped that we should be able to get safe ashore. I replied that there were no hopes of life, and, as we had all embarked in the same unhappy voyage, we would all take the same chance. I thought we ought to share the same fate. He said that should not be; and if I did not acquaint my people with their offer, I should have their lives to answer for.

In other words, claims the survivor Nichols (who is writing the history here), the Acadians begged their captors – the English captain and crew – to save themselves and leave the deported community to drown. Which is what happened. The *Duke William* went down with all the Acadians, bar Girard, who reached land with the English. It seems unusual that the captain and priest should be the first to leave a sinking boat. On the other hand, the Acadians could probably have overrun the crew if they'd wished. We'll never know what actually happened in those final moments on board the *Duke William*, but we do know that another tragic community of migrants, ripped from their homes, were left on board to drown together.

FELONS AWAY

As tiny England grabbed huge colonies, so it needed labour to exploit them. If there had been business schools in the 1800s, they would no doubt have praised plantation slavery. This brutal system helped to pioneer much of the efficiency and global links of industrial capitalism. Economically, however, it often made more sense to send white, rather than black, slaves: they spoke the language, required no detour to Africa for collection, and fewer died in transit.

That's why kidnapping was so popular. And why the Aberdeen magistrates turned a blind eye to Peter Williamson being taken at the age of eight [See *Spirited Away* above]. But private enterprise did not provide enough white labour and, in time, moral considerations were to reduce opportunities for the rich simply seizing whom they wished. So the government joined in by transporting its own ready supply of captives.

First this meant political prisoners. In 1649 Oliver Cromwell attacked Drogheda, a rich Irish town just north of Dublin. His troops killed 3,500 royalists and residents; any surviving garrison he sent to Barbados. Two years later, after the battle of Worcester, he shipped 1,610 Scottish prisoners to Virginia. In 1685, those supporters of rebellious Monmouth who escaped the hanging clutches of Judge Jeffreys were exported to America.

Next it was felons – and the net was cast wide. In one place in Dorset during the 18th century, you could be transported for merely damaging a bridge, or for stealing some bread. Minor crimes got seven years abroad, after which you had to pay your return passage. Serious crimes meant life. And even if you were freed and chose to stay abroad, you remained a second class citizen, unable, for example, to vote.

Those shipping the felons tended to be private contractors. Paid only for what they delivered alive, they balanced their desire to cram the holds with doing just enough to keep the prisoners breathing. George Selwyn MP reported with horror what he saw aboard a transport leaving for Maryland in 1767:

> *I went on board and all the horror I ever had an idea of is short of what I saw this poor man in; chained to a board in a hole not above 16 feet long, more than 50 with him, a collar and padlock about his neck and chained to five of the most dreadful creatures I ever looked on.*

From the great southern plantations to the emerging industrial centres, America cried out for more cheap labour than Africa could provide. So the trade in white convicts grew hugely in the 18th century. Slavers such as Jonathan Foreward diversified into transporting prisoners. They were guaranteed property rights over convicts, plus a subsidy of up to five pounds for each head they landed alive. Ireland stopped clearing so many Catholics and instead shed tens of thousands of felons and vagabonds.

Indentured servants often fared as badly as slaves; sometimes worse, as they could only be exploited during their term, whereas a slave could be worked for as long as they lived. John Lauson, transported for 14 years as a petty thief when he was 18, later wrote of his experiences in a mixed race plantation gang:

My European clothes were took from me, which never afterwards I could them see. A canvas shirt and trousers me they gave, a hop-sack frock, in which I was a slave; no shoes or stockings had I to wear, nor hat, nor cap, my hands and feet went bare, thus dressed unto the field I next did go, among tobacco plants all day to hoe. At day-break in the morn our work begun, and lasted till the setting of the Sun. My fellow-slaves were five transports more, with 18 negroes, which makes twenty-four. We and the negroes both

The Poor Unhappy
Tranſported Felon's
SORROWFUL ACCOUNT
Of his 14 Years Tranſportation at Virginia, in America.

In S I X P A R T S.

Being a remarkable and fuccinct Hiſtory of the Life of JOHN LAUSON, who was put Apprentice by his Father to a Cooper in the City of Briſtol, where he got into bad Company, and went a Robbing with a Gang of Thieves, but his Maſter got him back, yet he would not be kept from his old Companions, but went a Thieving with them again, for which he was tranſported 14 Years. With an Account of the Way the Tranſports work, and the Puniſhment they receive for committing any Fault. Concluding with a Word of Advice to all young Men to be upon their Guard, left they go through the Hardſhips he went through.

✳✳✳✳
✳✳✳
✳✳

BRIDGWATER: Printed by G. CASS, where Shopkeepers and Travellers may be ſupplied with Variety of Godly Books.

alike did fare, of work and food we had an equal share. At last it pleased God I sick did fall, yet I no favour did receive at all. Much hardship then indeed I did endure, no dog was every nursed so before; More pity the poor negro slaves bestow'd, than my inhuman brutal master show'd.

But by 1781 Britain had lost America and could no longer send prisoners there. The prison ships started backing up in the Thames. Welcome, Australia. And welcome a lot of lyrics about *10,000 miles* and *My love has sailed on a government ship.*

All Around My Hat

My love she was fair, and my love she was handsome
And cruel was the judge that sentenced her away
For thieving was a thing she never was inclined to
They sent my love across the sea ten thousand miles away.

> *All around my hat, I will wear the green willow,*
> *All around my hat for twelve month and a day*
> *And if anyone should ask me the reason why I'm wearing it*
> *It's all for my true love who is far, far away.*

Seven long years my love and I are parted
Seven long years my love is bound to stay
For seven long years I'll never be false-hearted
I'll never sigh or sorrow though she's far, far away.
> *All around my hat...*

Some young men are false and some they are deceiving
Seeking for some young girl they mean to lead astray
And when they have deceived them, so cruelly they'll leave them
I'll love my love forever though she's far, far away.
> *All around my hat...*

Jim Jones at Botany Bay

Come gather round and listen lads, and hear me tell my tale,
How o'er the sea from England I was condemned to sail.
The jury found me guilty, and says the judge, says he,
Oh for life, Jim Jones, I'm sending you across the stormy sea.

But take a tip before you ship to join the iron gang,
Don't get too gay in Botany Bay, or else you'll surely hang.
Or else you'll surely hang, he says, and after that, Jim Jones,
High upon yon gallows tree, the crows will pick your bones.

You'll have no chance for mischief there, remember what I say
Oh they'll flog the poaching out of you down there in Botany Bay.
With the storms a-raging round us, and the winds a-blowing gales
I'd rather have drowned in misery than go to New South Wales.

Our ship was high upon the seas when pirates came along,
But the soldiers on our convict ship were full five hundred strong;
They opened fire and soon they drove that pirate ship away
But I'd rather joined those buccaneers than go to Botany Bay.

Day and night in irons clad we like poor galley slaves
Will toil and toil our lives away to fill dishonoured graves;
But by and by I'll slip my chains and to the bush I'll go
And I'll join the brave bushrangers there, Jack Donahue and Co.

And some dark night when everything is silent in the town,
I'll get the bastards one and all, I'll shoot the floggers down.
I'll give them all a little treat, remember what I say,
And they'll yet regret they sent Jim Jones in chains to Botany Bay.

We don't know much about Jim Jones, the subject of this ballad, but we do know about his hero Jack Donahue. Donahue was a bushranger, a term first used for escaped convicts surviving in the Australian bush – and living by theft – but later extended to other outlaws and highwaymen such as Ned Kelly. As a gushing journalist wrote in *The Colac Herald*, Victoria on 8th April 1879:

Some seventy years ago in the sister colony of New South Wales ... a vessel with convicts arrived from England, having for one of its forced passengers a young man named Donahue. Born in Dublin and early thrown on the world an orphan, he had graduated in crime, from a pickpocket upwards, till a burglary in which he was concerned resulted in a sentence of transportation for life. His spirit was not tamed as was evident when on his first introduction to his cell in the prisoners' depot at Sydney, he exclaimed with great glee, 'A home for life'.

Donahue soon escaped and joined with other outlaws in a gang called The Strippers, known for stripping the rich of their possessions. There was a whiff of Robin Hood about him – as later with Ned Kelly – which Donahue fuelled with gratuitous brutality towards rich bullies. As the journalist continued:

He paid a visit to a station called Bogalong, belonging to a Mr Robertson, and on riding into the yard found that gentleman sitting in an easy chair, smoking and reading the paper while one of his men had been tied up and received severe lashes from a cat-o'-nine-tails. Ordering proceedings to be stopped, Donahue compelled the flagellator to unbind the floggee and, under penalty of immediate death, to put his master in his place.

Donahue's luck ran out in 1830 when he was shot dead by a soldier during a shoot out. His fame persists in the ballad *The Wild Colonial Boy* with his cry 'I'll fight but not surrender till I die'.

THE WOMEN OF THE FIRST FLEET

O ne fifth of the convicts first sent to New South Wales were women. If you were such a woman, what kind of voyage could you expect?

Convict ships tended to be smaller merchant vessels, converted from general cargo. Fees were low, so the ships were old and the crews were poor. But they weren't as bad as slave ships and they were a lot better than emigrant boats. Some convicts actually got healthier on board. Even so, the voyage was hardly fun.

In 1787 what became known as the First Fleet set sail for Australia. Now America was no longer a colony and able to receive convict labour, the British government decided to launch this new destination with 800 convicts, including 200 women and 14 children. A further 600 passengers and crew on board the inaugural fleet's 11 ships included soldiers, administrators and a selection of tradespeople to develop the colony. Even before they left Portsmouth, Captain Arthur Philip complained of the condition of the women prisoners:

> *The situation in which the magistrates sent the women on board the Lady Penrhyn stamps them with infamy – tho' almost naked, and so very filthy, that nothing but clothing them could have prevented them from perishing ... there are many venereal complaints, that must be spread in spite of every precaution I may take hereafter ... let me repeat my desire that orders immediately be given to increase the convict allowance of bread. 16lb of bread for 42 days is very little.*

We know about the women on the *Lady Penrhyn* because its surgeon, Arthur Bowes Smyth, kept a diary. The oldest aboard was 82-year-old Dorothy Handlyn, serving seven years for perjury. Most women convicts were transported for thieving: 21-year-old prostitute Mary Allen faced seven years for stealing from a client, while her accomplice Tamasin Allen was described as a 'lustyish woman with blonde hair'; 15-year-old Esther Abrahams, a milliner also convicted of theft, embarked with her baby daughter. Seven mothers brought children with them; thirteen women convicts gave birth during the eight-month voyage. Ten days from Portsmouth, Elizabeth Evans miscarried; a week later Isabella Lawson had a baby girl.

Once out of sight of land, all but the most troublesome were released from their chains and allowed to exercise on deck. This helped keep people alive, but still they lacked decent apparel. By the time they reached Rio, the women's clothing was infested with lice and had to be burnt. Instead they wore clothes made from rice sacks. Even so, they remained vulnerable to the advances of marines, crew and other convicts.

The surgeon Smyth describes their arrival at Botany Bay on Wednesday 6th February 1788, after thirteen months confined to the ship:

> *At five o'clock this morning, all things were got in order for landing the women. A search was made to see if any of the many things which they had stolen on board could be found, but their artifice eluded the most strict search, and at six o'clock p.m. we had the long-wished-for pleasure of seeing the last of them leave the ship. They were dressed in general very clean, and some few amongst them might be said to be well dressed. The men convicts got to them very soon after they landed, and it is beyond my abilities to give a just description of the scene of debauchery and riot that ensued during the night.*

Female Transport

Come all young girls, both far and near, and listen unto me
While unto you I do unfold what proved my destiny.
My mother died when I was young, it caused me to deplore
And I did get my way too soon upon my native shore.

Sarah Collins is my name, most dreadful is my fate,
My father reared me tenderly, the truth I do relate,
Till enticed by bad company along with many more
It led to my discovery, upon my native shore.

My trial it approached fast, before the judge I stood
And when the judge's sentence pass'd it fairly chill'd my blood
Crying you must be transported for fourteen years or more
And go from hence across the seas unto Van Diemen's shore.

It hurt my heart when on a coach my native town passed by
To see so many I did know, it made me heave a sigh,
Then to a ship was sent with speed along with many more
Whose aching hearts did grieve to go unto Van Diemen's shore.

The sea was rough, ran mountains high, with us poor girls 'twas hard
No one but God to us came nigh no one did us regard
At length alas we reached the land it grieved us ten times more
That wretched place Van Diemen's Land far from our native shore.

They chain'd us two by two and whipp'd and lash'd us along,
They cut off our provisions if we did the least thing wrong.
They march us in the burning sun until our feet are sore
So hard's our lot now we are got upon Van Diemen's shore.

We labour hard from morn to night until our bones do ache
Then every one they must obey, their mouldy beds must make.
We often wish, when we lay down, we ne'er may rise no more
To meet our savage governors upon Van Diemen's shore.

Every night when I lay down I wet my straw with tears
While wind upon that horrid shore did whistle in our ears.
Those dreadful beasts upon that land around our cots do roar
Most dismal is our doom upon Van Diemen's shore.

Come all young men and maidens do bad company forsake,
If tongue can tell our overthrow it would make your heart to ache.
You girls I pray be ruled by me, your wicked ways give o'er
For fear like us you spend your days upon Van Diemen's shore.

A welcome number of transportation ballads – such as this one – speak purely from the woman's perspective. And male stories often feature women aboard, for example: 'We had on board a lady fair, Bridget Reilly was her name, and she was sent from Liverpool for a-playing of the game. But the captain fell in love with her and he married her out of hand, and she proved true and kind to us going to Van Diemen's Land.'

REALITY

Part One of this book has told many tales of barbaric practices and lewd behaviour. We've just heard the story of the First Fleet, whose woman convicts landed in Australia into 'a scene of debauchery and riot'. These old reports and folk songs are interesting and often surprising but they are seldom, sadly, vivid. To shudder, you must read modern stories. Here is a horrific account from 1982 of Vietnamese refugees attacked by pirates.

As a girl in Vietnam, Hue was so cheerful that her mother would look at the smile and say, 'Rain or shine, the flower blooms'... That Hue can smile now, albeit with difficulty, is a tribute to the strength that made her one of the first women to captain a refugee boat. Her boat was 20 feet long and crowded with 33 refugees. The first two days of their voyage were uneventful, but at dusk on the third day, a large fishing boat appeared like a sinister shadow on the horizon and then bore down on them without a flag or lights. As they turned to avoid the boat, Hue ordered the women to smear their faces with engine oil and fish sauce to diminish their appeal. The ploy proved futile. The fishing boat easily caught up with them, and the first thing its crew did was demand that the women bathe. After bathing, the women were fed. After eating, they were searched. After being robbed, they were raped. Most of the crew members were dark skinned and curly haired. One who spoke English told Hue they were Cambodian, but she says that she did not believe him, that she thinks they were Thai. Their boat was distinctively Thai, and most of the pirates wore sarongs and headbands but no shirts, a common uniform for Thai fishermen. Hue shudders with disgust as she recalls the first man who raped her as 10 others clapped and cheered in a circle around them. His head was shaved, and the knife he held to her throat slashed her chin when she turned her head and clawed at his face. In retaliation, he and several other pirates clawed and bit her body with such force that she recently underwent surgery to reconstruct her mutilated breasts. The pirates then turned on a petite 16-year-old virgin and began to rape her as her father looked on. Unable to accommodate their brutality, the girl began to haemorrhage. As she slowly bled to death, they continued to rape her. After she died, they covered the upper half of their body with a sheet and raped her some more. By the time the pirates were finished with the girl, her father's eyes had seen more horror than his mind could handle. He had gone insane.

PART TWO

Duped or Desperate

I n which we meet a cast of poor unfortunates who ostensibly CHOSE to come aboard, but were mostly tricked or under duress in their passage as HUMAN CARGO.

People such as HUGH MACLEOD, who was slyly trapped into buying inaccessible land in Nova Scotia. And JONATHAN EDWARDS, crammed with a thousand other emigrants aboard a boat bound for New York. Not to forget the many, many victims of the lies of agent WILLIAM TAPSCOTT or the shameless dockside crimping in the port of San Francisco by the infamous SHANGHAI BROWN.

Emigrant ANN MCGINN was lost with her six children when their boat hit an iceberg, while ALEXANDER SETON drowned with his troops in perfect order upon the sinking deck of the *Birkenhead.*

And by most bitter of ironies, some of these PAYING passengers fared worse than those who had been violently enslaved. For once they'd paid, in advance, their Captain had little incentive to keep them alive. Truly the life of human cargo is harsh.

ADRIFT, ADRIFT

In the darkness far out to sea, Hashem Alsouki can't see his neighbours but he can hear them scream. They are two African women and Hashem lies on top of them. His limbs dig into theirs. They want him to move, but he can't – several people lie on top of him, with possibly more above. Dozens are crammed into this wooden dinghy. If anyone tries to shift, a smuggler kicks them back into place, fearing the boat might overbalance. All being well, they should reach Italy in six days. But for now, Hashem doesn't know if he'll survive the night. Suddenly, the person on his left vomits all over him. Hashem pays the favour forward, throwing up over the person to his right. He realises everyone is covered in sick. They have each paid $2,000 to spew over fellow refugees. Hashem left his home in Damascus in April 2012, three years earlier. All that remains of his house is the key in his pocket. The rest was blown up by the Syrian army.

Imagine for a moment you are such a refugee. You must leave all you know, taking only what you can carry. Your sole hope is somewhere you don't know, far away. To reach it, you must rely on people you do not trust. At the least you get bathed in vomit, at the worst you drown. And all along the way, people treat you as vermin.

Hashem Alsouki, the subject of that story, lived near Damascus with his wife and three children. One day in 2012 their quiet town started filling with armed men. It was not clear whether these were army, police or pro-regime militia. The armed men began destroying houses to create a buffer zone around Damascus airport, a few miles away. They also started seizing the town's men. Hashem was a civil servant who managed the payroll for the local water board. He had no idea how to go on the run. Do you? Their house was their savings, but the house was now rubble. The family managed to escape the armed men, sell their jewellery, get on a bus to Jordan, then a ferry to Egypt. There they got to a beach and joined a queue for a smuggling boat. Police arrived and arrested them. They missed the boat and spent eight days in jail, where they learnt that the boat they missed went on to sink, drowning its 500 passengers.

Out of jail the family had few options. They couldn't return to Syria, nor did they want to live indefinitely in a tent in Egypt. But neither could they put their children through the terror of another crossing. So mother and kids decided to stay in Alexandria while Hashem headed back to the beach, alone, where he joined another queue for another boat, just like the one that sank. He hoped to reach Sweden.

This story is not new. Let's go back two hundred years, to Scotland. Here too, many people are on the move. They're escaping famine, disease or landlords. And they're the prey of unscrupulous traffickers.

In 1800 a poster appeared across Highland towns:

NOTICE TO PASSENGERS
For
NOVA SCOTIA AND CANADA
A Substantial, Coppered fast sailing ship will be ready to receive passengers at Fort William on the 10th of June and sail for Pictou and Canada on the 20th. All those who wish to emigrate to these parts in Summer will find this an excellent opportunity, as every attention will be paid to the comfort of passengers, and they may depend on the utmost punctuality as the date of sailing. For particulars application may be made to Mr John Grant, Merchant in Fort William.

That sounds good, but how comfortable might the crossing actually be? We don't know what happened to Mr Grant's ship. But we do know what happened in the following year to the *Sarah* and the *Dove*, making the same journey from Fort William to Pictou in Nova Scotia. Into these two boats the agent George Dunoon crammed 700 people. If they had been African slaves, he could legally only carry 489 within such a volume of cabin. But he squeezed in one and a half times as many, even though these passengers were paying. On the *Sarah* alone, 49 people died during the trip. This level of mortality was not viewed as unusual.

THE BUSINESS OF CARGO

E vidence suggests that death rates were often higher on emigrant boats – whose passengers had volunteered, and paid, for their passage – than on slave ships. Clearly there was no moral equivalence in the suffering: emigrants who survived the trip were free, not slaves. But how could their crossing be so cruel?

As ever, it's a question of economics. Slavers only made money from cargo they delivered alive. But emigrants paid their passage in advance, so their carriers had no incentive to keep them breathing. Indeed, the more emigrants that died during a crossing, the more space and food available to the living. After a while ports such as New York started charging packet companies for the corpses they delivered, but the fines were no deterrent. Human cargo was too profitable.

In the 19th century the best cargo was carried in the soundest ships. The East India Company brought silk and tea and spices – light but costly goods – in the most technically advanced vessels of the age. But bulk commodities, high in weight yet low in value, did not need such quality of carriage. They didn't require such speed to get to market, nor such sturdiness to protect them against the elements.

The cheapest commodity was timber. It could even be carried in ships that leaked for, unlike virtually any other cargo, wood could survive a soaking. This enabled timber importers to choose the direst and most decrepit vessels off the scrap heap: those built from inferior wood such as spruce, or rundown veterans past their prime, their creaking hulls held together with chains. Timber ships were usually uninsurable. They needed only survive a couple of crossings to turn a profit; if they sank, the downside was limited. Their weakness was compounded by the poor quality of their crew, for only the reckless or incompetent would choose to work on such floating coffins.

Britain in the mid 1800s cried out for North American timber. But how could shippers fill the empty timber ships returning west to reload? The boats weren't fit to carry manufactured products, and the slave trade was abolished. So owners looked for another bulk, cheap commodity needing to go west, and found – emigrants.

The ships received little conversion to carry humans. Into the holds, still stinking of Canadian lumber and not high enough to stand up in, the owners would build two tiers of bunks. Each berth was roughly six foot by six foot – similar to a modern kingsize bed – but only 24–30 inches high. Into this tiny space would be bundled at least four people of any age or gender. With no privacy, space or sanitation, this was their world for the weeks of crossing.

The American novelist Herman Melville witnessed this as a sailor. He wrote:

'How, then, with the friendless emigrants, stowed away like bales of cotton and packed like slaves in a slave ship; confined in a place that, during storm time, must be closed against both light and air; who can do no cooking, nor warm so much as a cup of water; for the drenching seas would instantly flood the fire in their exposed galley on deck? We had not been at sea one week

when to hold your head down the hatchway was like holding it
down a suddenly opened cesspool.'

Though the press revelled in stories of shipwreck, the greatest
dangers lay on board. By 1819, emigrant boats were reaching
North America with as many as 10 per cent of their steerage
passengers dead from disease or starvation. Two decades later,
legislation demanded a minimum of 14 square feet per person,
with minimum weekly rations of water, biscuit and oatmeal. Yet
this didn't curb disease. In one month alone, November 1853,
29 emigrant ships left for America. Of their 13,762 passengers,
more than a third were attacked by cholera. Over a thousand died.

Her Bright Smile Haunts Me Still

It's been a year since last we met
And we may never meet again.
I have struggled to forget
But the struggle was in vain.
For her voice lives on the breeze
Her spirit comes at will;
In the midnight on the seas
Her bright smile haunts me still.
In the midnight on the seas
Her bright smile haunts me still.

I have sailed 'neath alien skies,
I have trod the desert path,
I have seen the storm arise
Like a giant in his wrath;
Every danger I have known
That a reckless life can fill;

Yet her presence is not flown
Her bright smile haunts me still
Yet her presence is not flown
Her bright smile haunts me still

At the first sweet dawn of light,
When I gaze upon the deep,
Her form still greets my sight
While the stars their vigils keep;
When I close mine aching eyes,
Sweet dreams my senses fill;
And from sleep when I arise,
Her bright smile haunts me still.
And from sleep when I arise,
Her bright smile haunts me still.

You can cross the world, but you can't escape. This 1864 song from the American South must have readily touched a nerve with immigrants. I imagine it sung by Irishmen freshly landed and sucked straight into the American civil war. Afraid and exposed, they might easily dwell on a love left behind or, more simply, a haunting memory of home.

FOUL AGENCY

O ne of the most notorious shipping agents was Mr William
Tapscott. From offices in Liverpool, Dublin and New York,
he fleeced those who needed to cross the Atlantic on the cheap.
There are many songs about his lies. Here's one of them, which
features the agent claiming his ship's in the dock taking in her
mail, suggesting she's a speedy mail packet. But no, she's actually
taking on bags of cheap 'meal' to feed the passengers.

Mr Tapscott

As I was a-walking down by the Clarence Dock,
I overheard an Irish girl conversing with Tapscott.
'Good morning Mister Tapscott, good morning, sir,' says she,
'O have you got a packet ship bound for Amerikee?'

'O yes, I have a packet ship, tomorrow she sets sail,
She's lying in the Waterloo Dock, taking in her mail.'
The day was fine when we set sail but night had barely come
That every emigrant never ceased to wish himself at home.

That night as we was sailing through the Channel of Saint James,
A dirty nor'west wind come up and blew us back again.
We snugged her down and laid her to with reefed main topsail set,
It was no joke, I tell you, 'cause our bunks and clothes was wet.

It cleared up fine at break of day, and we set sail once more,
And every migrant sure was glad to reach America's shore.
So now in Philadelphia I work on the canal,
To sail again in a packet ship I'm sure I never shall.

Tapscott's advertisements gushed gloriously:

*TO SAIL POSITIVELY ON THE 6TH AUGUST, the
magnificent new American Line Packet-ship CONSTITUTION,
2500 Tons Burthen. This splendid new Packet-ship is one of the
largest and most magnificent ships afloat, has three decks, and
fitted with every modern improvement for the comfort of
Passengers, which with Captain Britton's uniform kindness and
attention, should obtain for this noble ship a decided preference.
For terms of Passage, which will be moderate, early application
should be made to W. TAPSCOTT & CO., St. George's
Buildings, Regent Road, Clarence Dock, Liverpool.*

In reality, conditions for steerage passengers were mostly
disgusting. Ships seldom proved as large as promised, the food
was atrocious and disease most likely. When his eponymous ship
William Tapscott reached New York from Liverpool in October
1853, it bore 65 corpses, most dead from cholera or typhus.
Tapscott got his comeuppance in 1849 when he was declared
bankrupt and jailed for three years for fraud. But this is not likely
to have benefited the many thousands who had suffered on his
Atlantic crossings.

Where desperate families once flocked to Liverpool, they now
gather in places like Alexandria. In recent years, this Egyptian
port has become a giant holding bay for Syrians, Palestinians and
Africans seeking to cross the Mediterranean. Smugglers block-
book anonymous apartments, usually in exotically-named
suburbs such as Miami and Palm Beach. From there, the migrants
are bussed in curtained coaches to remote beaches at night. But
the vagaries of weather, tide and bribe-hungry officials mean few
embark on their first attempt. So they're bussed back to their
lodgings to try again another day.

It's unlikely their trafficker promises, like Mr Tapscott two centuries earlier, an easy and comfortable crossing. Most migrants today have smart phones. They know what awaits them. But when they pay the thousands of dollars demanded by the broker back in Aleppo, or Gaza City, they do at least expect to be delivered alive.

One of Tapscott's modern equivalents is a Syrian-Palestinian smuggling boss known as Abu Hamada. A shadowy figure, apparently once an engineer from Damascus whom many claimed to be linked to the Egyptian security services, Hamada ran two boats a week during 2015, earning £30,000 from each. Journalists linked him to some shocking allegations; for example, the fate of Wael Adeeb Shahwan, a 26-year-old Palestinian escaping Gaza in 2014. The smugglers stole his back pack, which contained the insulin vital for his diabetes. Days into the journey, as he slipped into a coma, they threw him overboard.

Another story linked to Hamada occurred in September 2014, when a ship sank off Malta drowning 300 people. Already four days at sea, it was met mid-ocean by its smuggler bosses in other boats. They demanded its captain transfer the already over-crowded cargo into a smaller vessel, less likely to be confiscated by Italian coastguards. The captain refused, saying that would sink the smaller boat. They threatened to kill his family. He stood firm. So the smugglers, laughing, rammed the boat and sped off. Most of those who drowned had been trapped below. Scores of survivors were picked up by a rescue boat. There had been 500 people aboard a boat no more than 20 metres long.

The emigrant tales from centuries ago are often shocking. But the world today – for all its transparency, high-tech communications and hunger for accountability – seems to have grown nastier.

AN IRISH COFFIN SHIP

Also known as the *Coughing Ships* for their chorus of wheezing consumptives, these cut-rate carriers provided a floating hell for poor emigrants escaping famine and clearance during the mid 19th century. They also carried first class passengers who, three times a day, wolfed down a meal that would have sustained someone in steerage for a week. One such luxury passenger in 1847 was Robert Whyte, who spent the long hours observing disease consume the ship:

Saturday 19th June. A shark followed us all the day and the mate said it was a certain forerunner of death. The cabin was like an apothecary's shop and the mistress a perfect slave. I endeavoured to render her every assistance in my power. The mate also was indefatigable in his exertions to alleviate the miserable lot of our helpless human cargo.

Tuesday 22nd June. One of the sailors was unable for duty and the mate feared he had the fever. The reports from the hold were growing even more alarming and some of the patients who were mending, had relapsed. One of the women was every moment expected to breathe her last and her friends – an aunt and cousins – were inconsolable about her as they had persuaded her to leave her father and mother and come with them. The mate said that her feet were swollen to double their natural size and covered with black putrid spots. I spent a considerable part of the day watching a shark that followed in our wake with great constancy.

Tuesday 6th July. During the past night there was a heavy fall of rain which left the atmosphere clear and cool. Two men (brothers) died of dysentery and I was awakened by the noise made by the mate, who was searching for an old sail to cover the remains with. In about an hour after, they were consigned to the deep, a remaining brother being the solitary mourner. He continued long to gaze upon the ocean, while a tear that dropped from his moistened eye told the grief he did not otherwise express. I learned in the afternoon that he was suffering from the same complaint that carried off his brothers.

Thursday 8th July. Another of the crew was taken ill, thereby reducing our hands when they were most required. The captain had a great dread of the coast of Newfoundland which, being broken into deep bays divided from each other by rocky capes, is rendered exceedingly perilous, more especially as the powerful currents set towards this inhospitable shore.

Friday 9th July. A few convalescents appeared upon deck. The appearance of the poor creatures was miserable in the extreme. We now had fifty sick, being nearly one half the whole number of passengers. The brother of the two men who died on the sixth instant followed them today. He was seized with dismay from the time of their death, which no doubt hurried on the malady to its fatal termination. The old sails being all used up, his remains were placed in two meal-sacks and a weight being fastened at foot, the body was placed upon one of the hatch battens from which, when raised over the bulwark, it fell into the deep and was no more seen. He left two little orphans, one of whom – a boy, seven years of age – I noticed in the evening wearing his deceased father's coat. Poor little fellow! He seemed quite unconscious of his loss and proud of the accession to his scanty covering. The remainder of the man's clothes were sold by auction by a friend of his who promised to take care of the children.

Wednesday 14th July. We had the bold headlands of Capes Gaspe and Rosier on our left and entered the majestic river St Lawrence which here, through a mouth 90 miles in width, after a course of *upwards of 2,000 miles, disgorges the accumulated waters of the great lakes. There was a birth on board this morning and two or three deaths were momentarily expected.*

Monday 26th July. After dinner, the mistress carried down to the cabin the baby that was born on board. The captain at first was very angry but a smile upon the face of the little innocent softened his heart and he soon caressed it with all the endearments he was in the habit of lavishing upon the canary.

Wednesday 28th July. Grosse Isle. The poor passengers, expecting that they would be all reviewed, were dressed in their best clothes and were clean, though haggard and weak. They were greatly disappointed in their expectations as they were under the impression that the sick would be immediately admitted to the hospital and the healthy landed upon the island, there to remain until taken to Quebec by a steamer.

The vast number of persons who quitted Europe to seek new homes in the western hemisphere in the year 1847, is without a precedent in history. Of the aggregate I cannot definitely speak but to be within the limits of truth, they exceeded 350,000. More than one half of these emigrants were from Ireland and to this portion was confined the devouring pestilence. The worse horrors of that slave-trade which it is the boast or the ambition of this empire to suppress at any cost, have been re-enacted in the flight of Irish subjects from their native shores. In only ten of the vessels that arrived at Montreal in July – four from Cork and six from Liverpool – out of 4,427 passengers, 804 had died on the passage and 847 were sick on their arrival. The Black Hole of Calcutta was a mercy compared to the holds of these vessels. Yet simultaneously, as if in reproof of those on whom the blame of all this wretchedness must fall, Germans from Hamburg and Bremen are daily arriving, healthy, robust and cheerful.

Not every ship was a killer. The *Jeanie Johnston* was famous for crossing the Atlantic 16 times, bearing more than 2,500 Irish emigrants, without the death of any passenger or crew member.

Built in Quebec in 1847 by noted shipwright John Munn, she was first intended to carry cargo, but the horrors of the Irish potato famine made emigration more urgent, and profitable. A one-way fare to Baltimore or New York then cost three pounds and ten shillings, several months' salary for a labourer, but often subsidised by a family member who had already emigrated.

But how did the *Jeanie Johnston* preserve life so much better than other emigrant ships? Her captain James Attridge was an Irishman with 28 years experience at sea, 20 of them as a captain. He was known for not overloading the ship. Her doctor, Richard Blennerhassett, another Irishman, was a well-connected professional who'd studied at Edinburgh, then one of the best medical colleges in Britain. He could have made much more money ashore, and lived more comfortably. But he chose to spend his adult life at sea. Blennerhassett's skills were central to the passengers' vitality. He left the boat in 1853 and died of cholera just a year later.

Neither, ironically, did the *Jeanie Johnston* survive long. She sank in 1858 while carrying timber from Quebec to Hull. But, true to her previous record, every person aboard was saved.

CANNIBALISM AFLOAT

O ne of the more horrific Atlantic crossings befell the 108 passengers who left Belfast on 31st July 1741 on board the *Seaflower*, bound for Philadelphia. First a storm broke the mast, then she was becalmed and started running out of food. Disease killed the captain and all the crew, except one. The remaining passengers bobbed around the mid-Atlantic without provisions or the means to sail. She was found sometime afterwards by another ship, the *Success*, whose ghastly discovery was reported in the *Pennsylvania Gazette* of 12th November that year:

> *They found the Body of a Man lying upon Deck partly cut up, and his Arm and Shoulder then boiling in a Pot, in Salt Water (which had been their only drink for a long Time), and so eager were the poor famish'd People for the Flesh of their dead Companions, that many of them had conceal'd Pieces of it in their Pockets, to eat as they had Opportunity.*

The *Seaflower* finally made it to Boston with 65 passengers, all barely alive. They had consumed six of their shipmates and were just cutting up their seventh when the spotted the *Success* coming to rescue them.

Here's a press report dated 4th November 2008:

It was only after two weeks at sea, his body dehydrated and near starvation, that Gregorio Maria Marizan finally took out his fisherman's knife. 27 migrants on the drifting boat had already died and when another man slumped over and stopped breathing, the 31-year-old knew he had to act. 'We cut from his leg and chest,' Maria Marizan told The Associated Press from a hospital in Providenciales in the Turks and Caicos. 'We cut little pieces and swallowed them like pills.' Maria Marizan and four others were the only survivors of the 33 Dominican migrants who had set out on the tiny, wooden vessel en route to Puerto Rico. The journey became a nightmare when both the boat's engines died. The captain disappeared in the darkness. Whether he swam off to find help or was thrown off by another passenger, Maria Marizan could not say.

AWFUL WRECK OF AN EMIGRANT SHIP

THE HEART-RENDING TIDINGS of the total wreck of the Hannah, freighted with nearly two hundred emigrants, bound for Quebec from Newry, was reported yesterday afternoon at Lloyd's. The unfortunate vessel, the Hannah, was a brig between 150 and 200 tons burden, belonging to Maryport and manned by a crew, it is said, of 12 seamen, under the command of Mr. Shaw, the master. On the 3rd of April last she sailed from Newry with the above number of emigrants on board. The emigrants chiefly consisted of agricultural labourers and their wives and children.

Armagh Guardian, 4th June 1849

Escaping the potato famine in Ireland, these poor emigrants from Warrenpoint and Newry were unlucky to be under the care of Curry Shaw, the 23-year-old Master of the *Hannah*. In the early hours of 29th April 1849, the ship struck an iceberg in the Gulf of St Lawrence and started sinking.

Shaw forced the ship's carpenter to lock the after hatch, condemning the passengers to death below. Another sailor freed them, at which point Shaw and his officers set off in the only lifeboat, threatening with swords any who tried to join them. Crew

members rushed to help the emigrants onto a neighbouring ice floe. Within 40 minutes the *Hannah* had sunk.

Of those who reached the ice, most were barely dressed in their night attire. An icy gale was blowing. John Murphy went to rescue his infant daughter but, while retrieving her from the water, lost his twin boys as the ice they stood upon drifted away. Ann McGinn managed to collect her six children, but all were to die as the frozen passengers spent a day out on the ice.

Late that afternoon, the barque *Nicaragua*, under Captain William Marshall, was surprised to find humans huddled upon a slender piece of ice and braved the iceberg to rescue them. It picked up 129 survivors. Between 50 and 60 were thought to have died, by drowning, frostbite or being crushed between the ice. As Marshall reported, 'No pen can describe the pitiable situation of the poor creatures, they were all but naked, cut and bruised, and frost-bitten.'

Ten days later the *Nicaragua* reached Quebec. Shaw and the officers, rescued by another boat, were charged with 'being guilty of one of the most revolting acts of inhumanity that can be conceived'. But it's thought that Shaw disputed the testimony of other survivors and avoided punishment.

NEW SCOTLAND

W hen summer smiles, the Scottish Highlands can be the finest place on earth. Maybe it was like that on 10th July 1773 as 190 emigrants – 33 families and 25 single men – boarded the *Hector* at Ullapool to head for a new life in Canada. If so, they might have wondered why they were leaving. The beauty of Loch Broom may, momentarily, have eclipsed the pain of poverty in semi-feudal Scotland or the humiliation of the Battle of Culloden 28 years earlier.

These emigrants had much to look forward to. In return for buying farm land as cheap as sixpence an acre, they'd been offered free passage and a year's free provisions. They were heading for a place called Pictou, high on the peninsula of Nova Scotia, 'New Scotland', that jutted out below Newfoundland. The agent promised them land 'with about twenty miles of sea coast ... bounded by two rivers on each side that run into it,' presenting opportunities for farming, timber and fishing.

It would have been simpler to migrate south to the industry of Glasgow, but there they might lose their culture. Highlanders liked to stick together, and this new land – though far away – offered the chance to rebuild their community in the Gaelic way to which they were accustomed.

Some worries must have crept in when they boarded the *Hector*. The hull of this old Dutch cargo ship was so rotten, one later wrote, 'the passengers could pick the wood out of her sides with their fingers.' As they were leaving:

A piper came on board who had not paid his passage; the captain ordered him ashore, but the strains of the national instrument affected those on board so much that they pleased to have him allowed to accompany them, and offered to share their own rations with him in exchange for his music during the passage. Their request was granted.

The crossing was hard. Smallpox and dysentery killed 18 of the children aboard. Food ran out and water was both scarce and foul. Passengers were soon searching out the mouldy oatcakes they'd discarded earlier on.

Hugh MacLeod, more prudent than the others, had gathered up the despised scraps into a bag. During the last days of the voyage his fellows were too glad to join him in devouring this refuse.

On reaching Newfoundland they met gales so severe the ship was blown two weeks off course. Finally, on 15th September, they approached Pictou Harbour. The piper donned the tartan now banned in Scotland, some of the men wore broadswords. They got ready to disembark.

But little they had been promised was true. Their allotted land was not easy and coastal, but miles inland within deep, uncleared forest. There were no provisions or shelter. It was too late to put down crops for the next year. And just weeks away was a winter far worse than any they'd ever seen. The situation was dangerous. Some chose to sell themselves as indentured servants; others tried to live on tree bark or clams and oysters prised from the ice. One group took arms to seize enough stock to keep themselves alive.

Meanwhile, back in Glasgow, the *Hector's* owner John Pagan sat comfortably. He'd got his nice fee, there was little chance of comeback, and little need to conceal his trickery. Even before the ship had left, a letter to the *Edinburgh Advertiser* had asked how 'a dreary tract of an uninhabited and uncultivated wilderness' could be 'of the smallest use', claiming 'this scheme will prove certain ruin to poor people'. But poor people did not read, and those who did read felt no need to act on their behalf.

MEDITERRANEAN REFUGEE DISASTER: 562 DROWNED

No, not 2016. This is 17th March 1891. The steamship *Utopia* heads from Trieste to New York with 815 impoverished Italian migrants squeezed into steerage. Captain John McKeague misjudges arrival in Gibraltar, piercing her hull on the iron bow of a British battleship. He launches the few lifeboats, but these are crushed by the ship as it turns over, then sinks within 20 minutes of the collision. 562 passengers and crewmembers drown, most trapped in the hold.

More than 16 million people left Italy during the 50 years straddling 1900. The poorer ones usually headed to North America and, as ever, were prey to the promises of agents and shippers. One regular ruse was to load the human cargo into old vessels designed to carry coal. In 1894 the journalist Ferruccio Macola described the smooth-tongued 'slave-traders', who were quite capable of loading 500 passengers into 500 cubic metres:

> *With the knife blade of competition they pare down the conditions of emigrants stowed in the cargo hold, like anchovies in tin cans, because their sheer number compensates the expenses. The steamers rigged by these greedy people become sinister ghost ships, which mark their slow path across the sea with a line of cadavers.*

A popular Italian song of the time told of a young woman asking her mother for 100 lire to go to America. The mother refuses, but the girl goes anyway and is drowned en route, re-inforcing as much *la maledizione della madre*, the mother's curse, as the migrant's eternal fear of the unknown.

Mamma Mia Dammi Cento Lire

Mamma mia dammi cento lire che in America voglio andar!
Cento lire io te le do, ma in America no, no, no.

> *Mother, give me one hundred lire as I want to go to America*
> *I will give you a hundred lire, but to America no way.*

Mamma mia dammi cento lire che in America voglio andar!
Cento lire e le scarpette, ma in America no, no, no.

> *Mother give me one hundred lire as I want to go to America*
> *Okay a hundred lire and shoes, but America no, no, no.*

I suoi fratelli alla finestra, mamma mia lassela andar.
Vai, vai pure o figlia ingrata che qualcosa succederà.

> *Her brothers at the window urge, Mother let her go.*
> *Go ahead, ungrateful daughter, for something bad will happen.*

Quando furono in mezzo al mare il bastimento si sprofondò.
Pescatore che peschi i pesci la mia figlia vai tu a pescar.

> *When they were at sea, the ship sank.*
> *O fisherman catching fish, go fish for my daughter.*

Il mio sangue è rosso e fino, i pesci del mare lo beveran.
La mia carne è bianca e pura e la balena la mangierà.

> *My blood is red and fine, the fish of the sea will drink it.*
> *My flesh is white and pure, the whale will eat it.*

Il consiglio della mia mamma l'era tutta la verità.
Mentre quello dei miei fratelli l'è stà quello che m'ha ingannà.

> *My mother's advice was completely true.*
> *But that of my brothers is what deceived me.*

HIRAETH

O n Sunday 25th May 1865, the 1,000 ton *Mimosa* left Liverpool with 153 emigrants aboard, aiming to create a Welsh community in Patagonia at the far tip of South America. One emigrant bore a letter from his uncle saying, 'Since you will not be dissuaded from expatriating yourselves to that wild outlandish desert ... if the Indians do eat you up, I can only wish them a confounded bad digestion.' Two months later they landed at Porth Madryn, near where a small Welsh-speaking population exists to this day.

Fewer emigrants left Wales than Scotland or Ireland, but those who did – some 60,000 between 1850 and 1870 – had similar reasons for leaving: poverty, eviction and a thirst for land and adventure. They were determined to preserve Welsh culture and non-conformism; hence the long public debates preceding the Patagonia venture; so also the antipathy of many Welsh emigrants towards Irish fellow travellers, whom they accused of being both papist and godless.

Jonathan Edwards wrote to his brother back in Wales with news about his crossing to New York in 1865:

> *On 4th April about a thousand people came aboard the ship, Welsh, English, Irish, German, French, and Dutchmen. We had dinner at about three o'clock, some kind of meat and potatoes but you at home often give better food to the pigs ... On 5th April there was nothing to be seen but people seasick. The breakfast that appeared was a strange sight, only a small loaf and a piece of butter the size of a robin's eye ... We arrived at Queenstown where from four to five hundred Irish were added to our number ... they took up everything ungodly like playing cards, dominoes, and every form of gambling and singing bawdy songs all the time. But when it became rough no one was so devoted and*

*made as many signs as they did, calling on the Virgin Mary ...
On 13th April two children were born today, one of whom no one
would own ...*

*14th April: Death is using his sword very easily now. Two died
last night and six today but I am of the opinion it is the lack of
food that is causing these deaths ... 17th April: The Germans
and the Irish have been drawing their knives on each other today
... 18th April: On one side of me there was a woman crying bitterly,
having seen her small baby thrown into the sea and she could not be
comforted. Even a twinge of pain frightens people now as they think
that it is the forerunner of cholera.*

The Welsh language contributes remarkably to the notion of emigration with the word *Hiraeth* (pronounced 'here-eyeth' with a well rolled 'r'). There's no direct translation in English. 'Homesickness' does not begin to convey what writer Pamela Petro describes as 'an unattainable longing for a place, a person, a figure, even a national history that may never have actually existed. To feel *hiraeth* is to feel a deep incompleteness and recognize it as familiar.' The Portugese have a similar word, *saudade*, which is sometimes translated as a feeling of longing, melancholy or nostalgia. Such darkness of spirit may abound among the Welsh and the Portugese, but surely is intrinsic to any community of human cargo.

LETTERS FROM LITTLE ENGLAND

B arely three miles long, one and a half miles wide, Alderney is a tiny English-speaking community on a rock off the coast of France. In mid 1939 Alderney received a handful of Jewish refugees from Germany. A year later, with invasion of the Channel Islands imminent, all the island's 1,500 population were evacuated, mostly to mainland Britain. Today, nearly 2,000 people live on the island. When in 2015 it was suggested that Alderney might welcome a few Syrian refugees, some islanders responded in similar fashion to 1939.

Letter to The Alderney Times, 9th June 1939:

*The World in general is deeply sorry about the plight of the
German and Austrian Jews and other victims of racial prejudice,
but surely the Society of Friends could have started their charity
nearer home. This Island has long wanted an influx of people to
swell its depleted population but there are thousands of British*

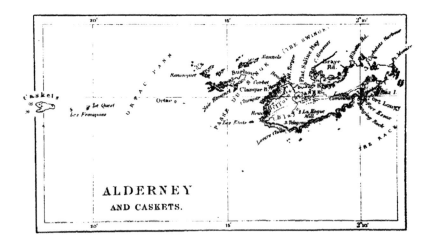

ALDERNEY
AND CASKETS.

unemployed who are deserving of Charity's first helping hand and a Colony of Jews is not likely to raise the standard of living in this island very much. Many of our readers have never had any dealings with Jews, or lived in their midst, but the writer has done both and is sorry that Alderney should have a number of them thrust upon her without the people being in any way consulted on the matter. The only consolation which is left to us is that they will not be with us very long.

Letter to The Alderney Press, 28th September 2015:

I am disgusted that the new States Member McKinley should show his ignorance by comparing the Evacuation of Alderney in 1940 with the present fiascos of rats leaving what they consider to be a sinking ship. In 1940 The British government told us we had to Evacuate, and they looked after us and took us under their wing, as best they could, like a Mother Hen, to somewhere within the realm. Our able bodied young men and women, did not jump on the first leaky boat available to run away like cowards, no, they enlisted in his Majesty's forces and fought for King and Country, making their contribution, and for many giving their lives. That is a vast difference from these cowards, who should be fighting to make their own country a fit place to bring up their families ... Does he not realize that this type of illegal immigrant brings with them all sorts of organised crime, i.e. prostitution, rape, burglary, drug lords, pickpocket etc, is this what he wants? ... If McKinley and his like minded friends want to help these people, they should go to the cowards countries, and help to make it fit to live in, so they will want to stay. There should be plenty of cheap property available. I don't apologise for this outburst it had to be said, why can't these people leave well alone.

THE BOUNTY

And it's over the mountain and over the main
Through Gibraltar, to France and Spain
Pit a feather tae your bonnet, and a kilt aboon your knee
Enlist my bonnie laddie and come awa with me.

T he British Army always needed men, but was more subtle than the Navy in recruiting them. It got people drunk, offered them a bounty, secured their signature and then whisked them away to serve the Crown, often across the world. This wasn't slavery as such, but it was a form of bondage, and of human cargo. The troopships were not fun: disease and transport killed as many soldiers as battle. Many songs tell of the sadness at losing a loved one who's bound to sail away. Not just sadness, but anger too – as shown by this great old folk song *The White Cockade*. A woman is furious with the man she loves who, full of drink and enticed by the King's shilling, must now take a ship far away.

The White Cockade

'Twas on one summer's morning as my love walked over the plain,
He had no thought of enlisting when a soldier to him came,
Who so kindly invited him to drink the ale that's brown,
He advanced him a shilling all to fight for the Crown.

So now my love has enlisted and he wears a white cockade,
He is a handsome young man, likewise a roving blade,
He is a handsome young man and he's going to serve the King,
Oh, my very heart is breaking all for the loss of him.

Oh, may he never prosper and may he never thrive
With anything he takes in hand, this world while he's alive,
May the very ground he walks upon, the grass refuse to grow,
Since he's being the only cause of my sorrow, grief and woe.

Some armies today resort to the press gang:

I was abducted in 1998. I was 9 years old. Six rebels came
through our yard. They went to loot for food. Its called 'jaja' –
'get food'. They said, 'We want to bring a small boy like you – we
like you.' My mother didn't comment; she just cried. My father
objected. They threatened to kill him. They argued with him at
the back of the house. I heard a gunshot. One of them told me,
'Let's go, they've killed your father.' A woman rebel grabbed my
hand roughly and took me along. I saw my father lying dead as
we passed. A, fourteen years old, Sudan.

As Peter Warren Singer wrote in his 2006 book *Children at War:*
'In many ways these tactics of abduction and impressment into
service echo the naval press gangs of the Napoleonic era.
However, the difference is not just the lower ages. Present-day
abduction raids are not only about building one's force, but are
also instruments of war in and of themselves ... designed to
intimidate local civilian communities.' He explains that 'during
the Ethiopian fighting in the 1990s, a common practice was that
armed militias would simply surround the public bazaar. They
would order every male to sit down and then force into a truck
anyone deemed eligible. This often included minors.'

In Syria's current civil war, the Assad regime has focused on
pressing troops from the president's own two-million-strong
Alawite community, whom it feels will fight most loyally. By spring
2015 it was estimated that one third of Alawite men of fighting
age had been killed. Many others had fled the draft as refugees.

DYING FOR THE DUTCH

*Most earnestly and emphatically do I commend these words to
the notice of my readers. Perhaps some of them are young men;
perhaps, under the pretext of seeing the world, and really in the
hope of amassing great fortunes, they are inclined to go to the
East Indies. If so, let them remember that in times of peace every
ship that leaves Holland for the East carries between 250 and
300 men, whereas the homeward-bound ships bring back only
one hundred. Where are the rest? My friends, out of every 100
men – especially if they be soldiers – who go to the East, seldom
more than 30 live to return. Out of every 100 men who remain
in the East, seldom more than ten obtain promotion or are
employed in a service that enables them to earn a decent living.
Out of a 1,000 men who did obtain promotion you would
seldom – very seldom – find a single one who had experienced
good fortune, and who returned to Europe a rich man.
Remember these things, my friends, and do not go to the East.*

S uch was the advice given by O. F. Mentzel, a German soldier
who sailed to the Cape of Good Hope in 1732. Like half a
million other German emigrants, he'd signed up with the Dutch
East India Company (known as the VOC) for service out East. The
Dutch were as canny as their population was tiny. They used
foreigners to protect and work their colonies in the Cape, Ceylon,
Batavia (Indonesia) and elsewhere. And that labour, mainly poor
Germans, came willingly, offering up to five years' bondage in
return for very little.

Mentzel detailed the cruel economics. Volunteers would be
snapped up by the VOC's recruiting agents, known as *zielverkopers*
or 'soul purchasers'. Each recruit started with a debt of 172
gulden: 150 for clothing and equipment, 22 for two and a half
month's pay in advance, little of which they actually received. 'All

this has to be earned and paid off bit by bit. Other amounts, moreover, are from time to time added to the original sum, and the whole debt can scarcely be paid off in less than five years.'

But people were desperate. It's estimated that nearly one in three of the adult German-speaking population in Europe – some 15 million in total – migrated during the 17th and 18th centuries.

Any initial optimism would soon be tested aboard the VOC transport ships. Mentzel described how the soldiers would be piled on top of each other to fit into the tiny, airless space between decks. The 'exudations from so many person sleeping close together, in whose stomachs indigestible food ingredients are putrefying, the evil smelling or, worse still, acidifying water, and the constantly moist sea air cause, all too soon, diseases which usually attack the newly enlisted men first.'

Sailing to the Cape took between four and five months. The best recruits were chosen to stay there – a relatively benign posting. The rest would journey a further three months to the Far East. Newcomers thought that if they could survive the voyage, they'd survive the indenture. But worse was to come. Batavia was full of typhoid, malaria and dysentery which, each year, killed more Europeans than could be replenished by the mighty VOC fleets. In the late 18th century, only one in ten Dutch soldiers returned from Southeast Asia, much worse than Mentzel's estimate.

Where there are sailors, there are shanties – and many songs survive from the Dutch fleets. In *Matroos Af-Scheyt*, 'Sailor's Farewell', a young man glamorises the adventurers returning from the East. When the women in his life – his mother, his neighbours – warn him against embarking on such a dangerous voyage, he hunts out reasons to ignore them:

Ick siese uyt en t'huys komen hier,
Zy drincken, sy klincken, sy maeken goet chier,

Zy syn in 't habyt,
Gekleedt met zijd'.
Ick moet mee gaen varen, dat is myn vlyt.

I see here departures and arrivals,
They drink, they toast, they cut a dash,
They have silk clothes on.
I have to sail with them, that's what I want.

Then the girls will come and make me afraid,
They say: 'Boy next door, how could you sail away from home
for so long? You're making a mistake,
You will one day say: Oh! If only I were home.'

As I laugh, I say: 'Girls, keep quiet,
I sail because I don't want you;
even if we sail far away, we will return,
then we can choose the girls.'

IN PERFECT ORDER AS THEY DROWN

F amine forced over a million people to flee the potato blight of the 1840s in Ireland and Scotland. Most braved the crossing to America, but some young men preferred the harsh security of the British Army. Soon after receiving their boots and uniform, many of these new recruits were rushed, untrained, aboard troopships to fight for the Queen in South Africa.

One such troopship was the *Birkenhead*, which left Queenstown in Ireland during January 1852, straight into a winter storm that killed some and injured many among those crowded below. Conditions improved and the ship reached Cape Town. But there was no chance for leisurely disembarkation of the sick and injured: the Kaffir campaign was going badly, so the *Birkenhead* set off rapidly for Port Elizabeth, heaving with 638 officers, men, women, children and horses. Eight hours later she struck a reef off the aptly named Danger Point. Seawater swiftly drowned those crowded below. Up on the deck of the listing vessel, Major Alexander Seton of the 74th Highlanders ordered his soldiers to form rank. In silence, they watched the women and children – their families – embark in the few lifeboats. They saw the horses blindfolded and driven into the sea, to be attacked at once by sharks. The officers shook hands and resumed their position. The troops remained in ranks as they were engulfed by the waves. Some survived by clinging to the mast, which remained above the surface. Some even escaped sharks and strong currents to reach the shore several miles away. But 445 were lost.

The story of the *Birkenhead* is held up as one of the most gallant tales of the British Army; the origin of *Women and Children First*. But from Neptune's perspective, it was another delivery of human cargo to the deep.

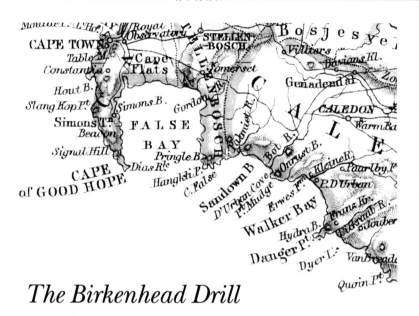

The Birkenhead Drill

To take your chance in the thick of a rush, with firing all about,
Is nothing so bad when you've cover to 'and, an' leave an' likin'
to shout;
But to stand an' be still to the Birken'ead drill is a damn tough bullet
to chew,
An' they done it, the Jollies - 'Er Majesty's Jollies - soldier an' sailor too!
Their work was done when it 'adn't begun; they was younger nor me
an' you;
Their choice it was plain between drownin' in 'eaps an' bein' mopped
by the screw,
So they stood an' was still to the Birken'ead drill, soldier an' sailor too.

Rudyard Kipling

THE UNION ARMY RECRUITS IN IRELAND

The flood of famine-fleeing Irish immigrants to North America receded during the late 1850s; by 1861 the flow had even reversed, as the horrors of the American Civil War drove migrants back to the home country. But two years later, though the war was bloodier than ever, immigrant numbers shot back up to 100,000. Two factors lay behind this. The first was railways.

There was a race to build track towards the nation's centre from either side, but the mighty railway companies were having trouble persuading enough Americans to endure the dangerous drudge of building new line. Out west, they shipped in Chinese labour. In the east, they looked to Ireland. They sent agents across the Atlantic to the impoverished hordes on the edge of old Europe, promising high wages, short contracts and free land afterwards. The railway companies worked closely with the shipping lines: immigrants would get a seemingly free crossing, then, before they could leave the boat, they would be forced to sign work contracts that paid for their passage over a term of up to five years. It was all legal. Indeed US law required shippers to ensure arrivals did not burden the state, so the agents would not let immigrants leave the boat until they signed.

The second magnet was war. Unlicensed military recruiters from the northern states started appearing in Ireland. They promised bounties to young men prepared to contract their labour; in this case their labour being to soldier for the Union. So many recruits came this way that the southern Confederacy asked the Vatican to instruct Irish Catholics not to join the northern army. The British government echoed these concerns as it, and the powerful British railway companies, feared the haemorrhaging of cheap Irish labour across the Atlantic.

Even so, many young men from Galway and Sligo soon found themselves on the battlefields of Gettysburg and Cold Harbor. And many regretted it, as was shown by the popular song *Paddy's Lamentation*, also known as *By the Hush*.

By the Hush

And it's by the hush, me boys
And be sure to hold your noise,
And listen to poor Paddy's lamentation.
For I was by hunger pressed,
And by poverty distressed,
And I took a thought I'd leave the Irish nation.

    Oh you boys, now take my advice;
    To America I'd have you not be coming
    For there's nothing here but war,
    And the thundering cannons roar,
    And I wish I was back home in dear old Ireland.

I sold me horse and plough,
Me little pigs and cow,
And me little farm of land and I were parted.
And me sweetheart, Bid McGhee,
I'm sure that I'll never see,
For I left her there that morning, broken hearted.
    Oh you boys, now take my advice...

It was me and a hundred more,
To America sailed o'er,
Our fortunes to be made, so we were thinking;

But when we got to Yankee lands,
They shoved a gun into our hands,
Saying, 'Paddy, you must go and fight for Lincoln.'
　　Oh you boys, now take my advice...

General Meagher to us said,
'If you get shot or lose a leg
Every mother's son of you will get a pension'.
But in the war I lost me leg
And all I got's this wooden peg;
Me boys it is the truth to you I mention.
　　Oh you boys, now take my advice...

Now I think meself in luck
To be fed upon Indian buck
In old Ireland, the country I delight in;
And with the devil I do say,
'Curse Americay,'
For I'm sure I've had enough of their hard fighting.
　　Oh you boys, now take my advice...

Little changes. Under the gloriously-named programme, Military Accessions Vital to the National Interest, today's US Army fast-tracks citizenship to immigrants with language and medical skills – provided they join up and fight. Recently the Pentagon reported that 65,000 green card holders serve in this way. But when they return after years of service in, say, Iran or Afghanistan, many don't actually get their citizenship – and can be legally deported for minor offences like drink-driving. Many veterans, particularly of Mexican origin, have been expelled in this way. It's an injustice not lost on those who remember the civil rights movement was spurred, in part, by African American veterans returning from World War Two to find their status still unequal.

THE DOCKSIDE CRIMPS

So the navy had the press gang, the army had the bounty. What about the merchant fleet? Packet ships also needed sailors, but had no right to press men – so they got crafty, like the army. They used dockside 'crimps', aggressive recruiters who fooled naïve landsmen into a life afloat, or simply drugged them with doctored whisky. Famous crimps included Paddy West in Liverpool and Shanghai Brown in San Francisco.

Cicely Fox Smith wrote a great poem about Shanghai Brown in San Francisco:

Shanghai Passage

'Shanghai Brown, Shanghai Brown!'
The Skipper o' the Harvest Moon is rampin' round the town
Looking for some sailormen to beg or steal or borrow –
Can't get a crew an' he wants to sail tomorrow!
'Prime seamen's very scarce just now – let him put his money down,
An' I'll see what I can do for him,' says Shanghai Brown.

'Shanghai Brown, Shanghai Brown!'
He's sent his touts an' runners out all around the town;

He's raked in men both high an' low, he's got both black an' white;
He's got the Lauderdale's port watch that only berthed last night;
He's got a brace of farmhands with the hayseeds in their hair;
He's got a bridegroom and best man, for what does Shanghai care?

An' he's shipped 'em in the Harvest Moon, the toughest packet goin',
(That never gets a sailorman to sign aboard her, knowin'),
With a hardcase drivin' skipper, an' a bull-voiced bucko mate,
By the Shanghai passage from the Golden Gate.

They'll be wonderin' in the mornin' what it was they drank las' night;
They'll be wonderin' what's hit 'em if they show an ounce of fight;
They'll be scoffin' seaboot duff, they'll be suppin' handspike gruel,
An' dodgin' the belayin'-pins, and cursin' Shanghai cruel;

But there's one won't wake nor wonder, nor scoff no grub at all,
Nor drag his achin' bones along to tally on the fall,
Nor jump to please the toughest mate New England ever bred,
Not stand no trick nor lookout – an' for why? Because he's dead!

'Shanghai Brown, Shanghai Brown!'
The Skipper o' the Harvest Moon is rampin' round the town,
Looking for some sailormen to beg or steal or borrow –
Can't get a crew an' he wants to sail tomorrow!
'Prime seamen's very scarce just now!,' says Shanghai Brown,
So he's took an' shipped a corpse away, has Shanghai Brown,
By the Shanghai Passage, outer 'Frisco Town!

[*Ramping* is another word for rampaging; *seaboot duff* means being beaten up; *handspike gruel* is a euphemism for blood; *to tally on the fall* is to grab and haul a line.]

RUSHING FOR THE GOLD

G old transformed Australia. When first found there in 1851, it triggered a decade-long flood of immigrant fleets. The population of the new nation tripled, with Victoria's inhabitants rising six-fold from 80,000 to 540,000 in just two years. Most arrived from the UK, some from mainland Europe and America, and a significant but spectacularly-abused minority from China. The railway and telegraph grew fast to support the arrivals. The camaraderie of those working on the goldfields propelled the words 'digger' and 'mateship' into the Australian psyche. As Henry Lawson wrote in *The Roaring Days*, 1889:

> *The night too quickly passes*
> *And we are growing old,*
> *So let us fill our glasses*
> *And toast the Days of Gold;*
> *When finds of wondrous treasure*
> *Set all the South ablaze,*
> *And you and I were faithful mates*
> *All through the roaring days.*

These new immigrants were more middle class than the convicts coming before – and better-heeled than the migrants heading elsewhere: only a third of adult males were classified as labourers, compared to 60% of those leaving for America at the time. Convict transportation petered out as the British authorities saw no point in paying free passage to potential gold miners. The introduction of more tradespeople and professionals helped fashion the emerging nation. Few had their financial dreams met by gold-mining, but many were no doubt pleased with the brasher, more egalitarian way of living.

Prior to the Gold Rush, the boats taking convicts or emigrants to Australia had death rates of around 2.3%, which was low for the time. But once passenger numbers increased, the death rate rose to 5%, even despite technical improvements, quicker sailing times and advances in hygiene. Free markets seldom factor in safety, unless they're forced to.

But while more died, the survivors arrived quicker. Speeding their arrival was that marvel of American ship design – the clipper, which cut the trip from England to Australia to as little as 64 days. The Yankee clipper was long and fast. It had a narrow hull, sharp bow and three tall masts sporting acres of canvas.

In March 1853 the *Marco Polo*, a Canadian-built clipper once reckoned the 'fastest ship in the world', left Liverpool for Melbourne. On board was a single young Englishman called Edwin Bird, who kept a diary of the journey. From it emerges a journey not without violence and pain, but also full of music, fun and hope.

She hauled out of the Salt House dock on Wednesday the 9th March 1853 at half past ten o'clock in the morning. There was a nice band on board and just as her noble stern was clearing the dock gates they struck up The Girls We Left Behind Us but it did not take any effect on me. She lay in the river until Sunday morning when she weighed anchor, fired four salutes and was answered by the American mailship Niagara and went beautifully down the river amidst the cheers of thousands of spectators.

Our first day of Sailing was Sunday the 13th. The tug took us not far over the bar as the wind was blowing nicely down the river. When the tug left, we gave her two more cannons and as many Huzzars as the lungs of the Marco Polo would permit. I slept on board last night for the first time but not so comfortable as I could wish. We found one stowaway just in time to send him back with the tug.

Wednesday 23rd March. The Captain went round last night at 11 o'clock to see things all right. He found one of the stewards very tipsy and saucy with it. He took a lamp from a passenger's Hand and floor'd him with it. He looked quite a member of Eton College this morning. The wind has been contrary all day. We have had no music; whist, draughts and chess with cribbage being the order of this wet day.

Thursday 24th March. Going 10 knots an hour all day, S.W. by W. A beautiful day quite a summer's one. The band played on deck this afternoon. A little boy died this morning and I have just seen him thrown overboard.

Monday 28th March. We are now in the trade winds which are very steady as yet. Are going about 6 knots an hour. A lovely day, steering S.W. by W. The band on deck this afternoon. There was a tremendous row last night between the Irish ladies and some of our passengers. They came on board as widows of officers and gentlemen's daughters. Surprised at hearing the noise so late, I jumped out of my bunk and to my surprise one of those ladies was swearing away and challenging to fight any man on board the Marco Polo. They are about all night long and some of the moonlight meets are queer ones to tell, I can assure you. The Captain has, through the advice of his good lady, put up a notice on the poop cabin today, that no ladies are to be on deck after 10 o'clock without being accompanied by their husbands, which of course no respectable female would do, and Mrs Forbes declared she would not walk the deck if such lounging about on the poop was not stopped.

Tuesday 29th March. I gave my money and watch and insurance in the Captain's hand, as he said it was not safe in my berth, so now I have not so much on my mind. One passenger was lashed to the rigging this afternoon for not paying his fine. There has been a fight just now in the 3rd Cabin between some of the Tipperary Boys, which are Cases ... The young woman I spoke of being ill the other day, or frightened, died a few minutes ago and a happy release for the poor creature and her friends. A very nice young fellow was took seriously ill last evening and he's not expected to live. I have played many a rubber of whist with him since on board.

Wednesday 30th March. The young woman was thrown overboard about an hour after her decease. She did not sink through carelessness in not putting in enough holy stone. She was seen last floating on the waves towards the coast of Africa

where, if a shark should not swallow her, she might possibly be buried in the land. The young man is much better but a little out ... we are now going at a spanking rate of 14 knots, all sails set.

Tuesday 5th April. We caught a shark this afternoon and while I was taking the hook from its mouth it bit my thumb – there was a great many dolphins and pilot fish and a shark in sight. My thumb was sore. I have had it dressed. A very hot day. The band has been playing.

Wednesday 6th April. Very warm all night with a squall in the morning at daybreak with rain in torrents. Good fun to see the people running down with their beds that had been on deck all night. A vessel in sight from London. As we were both in a calm we lowered a boat and boarded her about 5 miles off. She had a Dutch crew with only 28 passengers bound for Melbourne, and they made up a party and came on board the Marco Polo and dined with us and stayed until 6 o'clock and since it was such a treat to see so many different faces and to hear such a nice Band as ours was, they all got pretty tight before leaving and had to pull back in the dark. One cabin passenger, Mr Gardener, got put in chains for the night. He threatened to shoot the Captain and insulted Mrs Forbes and several of the passengers. We are knocking about in a dead calm.

Friday 8th April. A vessel was seen coming towards our bows and the Captain fancied she was homeward bound. Ordered a mail bag to be put on the poop directly for the reception of letters, which caused a deal of excitement. I did not write as no news is good news. When it was cleared I should say there was more than 500 letters and very likely 1,000 in it.

Wednesday 13th April. We are now in the S.E. Trades. Very hot and the passengers likewise.

Saturday 16th April. Rather hot. A few fights and music closed the day.

Saturday 23rd April. Going 12 knots nearly all day. Held a court martial on the Irishman. Was on the Jury. We found him guilty.

Was sentenced to 9 days in irons and kept on bread and water. A very wet afternoon. Music and singing in the cabin and a cold evening. We are now south of the Cape of Good Hope.

Wednesday 27th April. A gale and a heavy sea which made us roll awful. Upsetting soup, breaking legs, heads and so forth. Passengers tumbling from one end of the deck to the other. Fights and Rows are the order of the day. All through whiskey ... the man that broke his leg died on Sunday from the effects of it and was buried the same evening. This has been a very quiet week as regards rows. We have been more happy together. We were out 8 weeks on Sunday.

Wednesday 18th May. The thermometer stands 30 on deck this morning. Decks covered with snow and bitter and cold this morning. Snowballing the order of the morning.

Sunday 22nd May. We saw a very large Iceberg on Sunday, about 10 times as big as the Marco Polo.

Saturday 28th May. The first vessel we had seen for a month or 5 weeks was quite cheering. She proved to be the Halifax from London, 116 Days out and the Dutch captain was quite flabbergasted when he was informed we were out only 73 days ... Hobson's Bay at 2 o'clock on the Sunday amidst the deafening cheers of the crew and passengers, thus ending one of the quickest passages on record, beating his last voyage by a few hours only ... Melbourne is now in sight, and quite a sight to see the tents pitched along the beach. The country appears very level and very green considering it's now within three weeks of the midst of their winter. We all go ashore tomorrow in hope of getting hold of some dust as there is good news from Melbourne and the diggings.

Grimy men huddle around a fire. Worn by a hard day's panning, they listen to a tune picked out on a five-string banjo, then hear a singer tell a story they all know: the passage to California may have been tough, but it prepared them for the hardship ahead.

When James W Marshall found gold in Coloma, California on 24th January 1848, the news drew 300,000 gold-seekers to this distant spot. Some crossed the country by covered wagon, but many came west by sailing ship, enduring crush, bad food and the terror of rounding the Horn. This song features an extra, unpalatable detail: swallowing pork rind, tied to a string for retrieval, was an infamous cure for seasickness.

Coming Around the Horn

Now miners, if you'll listen, I'll tell you quite a tale,
About the voyage around Cape Horn, they call a pleasant sail;
We bought a ship, and had her stowed with houses, tools and grub,
But cursed the day we ever sailed in the poor old rotten tub.

Oh, I remember well the lies they used to tell,
Of gold so bright, it hurt the sight, and made the miners yell.

We left old New York city, with the weather very thick,
The second day we puked up boots, oh, wusn't we all sea-sick!

I swallowed pork tied to a string, which made a dreadful shout,
I felt it strike the bottom, but I could not pull it out.

We all were owners in the ship, and soon began to growl,
Because we hadn't ham and eggs, and now and then a fowl;
We told the captain what to do, as him we had to pay,
The captain swore that he was boss, and we should him obey.

We lived like hogs penned up to fat, our vessel was so small,
We had a 'duff' but once a month, and twice a day a squall;
A meeting now and then was held, which kicked up quite a stink,
The captain damned us fore and aft, and wished the box would sink.

Off Cape Horn, where we lay becalmed, kind Providence seemed
to frown,
We had to stand up night and day, none of us dared sit down;
For some had half a dozen boils, 'twas awful sure's you're born,
But some would try it on the sly, and got pricked by the Horn.

We stopped at Valparaiso, where the women are so loose,
And all got drunk as usual, got shoved in the Calaboose;
Our ragged, rotten sails were patched, the ship made ready for sea,
But every man, except the cook, was up town on a spree.

We sobered off, set sail again, on short allowance, of course,
With water thick as castor oil, and stinking beef much worse;
We had the scurvy and the itch, and any amount of lice,
The medicine chest went overboard, with bluemass, cards and dice.

We arrived at San Francisco, and all went to the mines,
We left an agent back to sell our goods of various kinds;
A friend wrote up to let us know our agent, Mr. Gates,
Had sold the ship and cargo, sent the money to the States.

FINAL VOYAGE

This book has chronicled the horrors of human cargo, of people treated as products or animals. It closes with a different tale – of precious human cargo, carried with care.

It was the body of Horatio Nelson, an Englishman who had lived all his life for one moment – to steer Britain to mastery of the waves – and when that moment came, at the Battle of Trafalgar mid afternoon on 21st October 1805, he was killed.

At 1.15pm a bullet from a French sharpshooter on board the *Redoutable* hit the admiral as he stood upon the quarter deck of the *Victory*. It shattered his shoulder, lung and spine. Knowing he would not survive, Nelson was taken down to the dark cockpit where the other wounded lay. Two hours later, on hearing Captain Hardy's news that 14 enemy ships had been captured with no British loss, he said: 'Thank God I have done my duty.' By 4.30pm, he was dead.

Nelson's body was stripped, shaved and placed within the largest barrel that could be found. More than a hundred gallons of brandy were poured over it. The barrel was sealed and set upon the middle gun deck of the *Victory*, guarded by marines. Terrible winds threatened its seven-day journey to Gibraltar. There the brandy was drained off and replaced with a solution of two parts brandy and one part spirit of wine.

On 4th November, the *Victory* set sail for England. Those on board must have had mixed feelings. They'd survived the carnage of Trafalgar, but lost good friends. Peace beckoned, but peace meant poverty for most at sea. They'd been part of the greatest sea battle of their lifetime and they carried the news and spoils of victory. But their vessel was a hearse – and it bore the body of one of England's greatest sons.

Mike O'Connor has written a song about this journey. 'I imagined,' he explains, 'Nelson's spirit directing the voyage, recalling his old battles.'

Carrying Nelson Home

Ease the bow spring.
Gently set the foresheets on the windward side.
Let go fore and aft, and as she turns
Sail her full and bye to catch the evening tide.
Shake out those topsails.
Feel the seas roll under that she knows so well
Find a star to guide her to the dawn.
And then let her greet the long Atlantic swell.

> *Sing me a shanty,*
> *Canta del cabo San Vicente,*
> *Chantez des marins du Nile,*
> *Sing a hymn of Trafalgar.*

Stream the log now,
For she's heeling with a land breeze to inspire
Orange-scented from the groves of Andalusia.
And within my mind Cadiz still gleams with fire.
Give her sea room.
Put St. Vincent well astern by break of day
Then shorten sail and harden up those sheets,
And close hauled we'll make the northings slip away.
  Sing me a shanty...

One point to leeward,
For the rolling seas are getting shorter now,
They remind me of the lights of far Hyeres,
And they tell me Biscay's on the starboard bow.
Shake out your reef.
For carried on the breeze that's setting fair
Are spices from the quays of Lorient,
You can sail her free to weather Finisterre.
  Sing me a shanty...

Ease your main sheets,
For it's soon we'll see the harbour lights of home.
Anchor, make-good every sheet and halliard.
Remembering just who you have on board.
Pipe me ashore,
Gently hoist aloft your keg of brandy wine.
Make ready to receive the admiral's barge.
Lower me easy, I'm going ashore one last time.
  Sing me a shanty...

INDEX OF SONGS

Welcome to the arcane but absorbing world of traditional song. Most songs in this book have no single recognised writer or tune. They were passed down orally, each singer hearing them sung, taking a fancy and learning the words for themselves. Along the way, the songs might mutate as singers wrote fresh lines or inserted verses from elsewhere. Local entrepreneurs would publish versions as broadsides: cheap songsheets sold in the street. In time, collectors would fish out the songs from that old woman in the village – last link to the oral tradition – or through moth-eaten broadsides from the junkshop or the Bodleian Library. Today, there are armies of amateur sleuths, who love tracking the precise genealogy of lyrics. Many's the time someone has collared me in a folk club saying, 'That ballad you just sung, you know you got the third line of the fourth verse wrong...'

The online home of these experts is mudcat.org, aka *The Mudcat Café*. Here you'll find decade-long discussions of single ballads. It's a wonderful community and resource. Another fine place is mainlynorfolk.info – a warren of nutritious detail about songs and recordings. And as big libraries share more online, it's easier to view original broadsides and songsters. That's how I found the obscure gem about the Gold Rush *Coming Around the Horn*.

One of the best online resources is The Full English – a recent gift from the English Folk Dance and Song Society (EFDSS). You can browse not just thousands of songs but also dances, tunes and customs, gathered by great English collectors like Cecil Sharp, Lucy Broadwood and Ralph Vaughan Williams. Say, for example, you're interested in the song *All Around My Hat*. Within seconds of entering The Full English you can view an original early Victorian printing of a music hall song of that title – featuring spoken cockney asides such as *She had a nice wegitable countenance*, *turnip nose, redish cheeks and carotty hair* and *Here's your valnuts, crack 'em and try 'em, a shilling a hundred.* These jokey street cries bear little relation to the song sung today, but they bring odour of the well from which it sprung.

Of course, you don't have to be a trainspotter to love travel. This world is open to all. Why not see what songs or stories take your fancy, then follow where they lead? As I hope this book shows, it's never just about the song.

I've deliberately not given music or chords, as these can put off non-musicians (and are easy to find online). I'd rather present the popular songs – the survivors – as true words of the people: storied thoughts whose genetic vigour has enabled them to survive the crowd's indifference and to entice singer after singer to make them their own.

Many songs could command their own chapter of provenance: try browsing discussions about *John Kanaka* or *Amazing Grace.* I have sought to be accurate, and to summarise judiciously where there is acres of debate, but this index may still contain mistakes. For which, apologies. But if you want to dig, you've got to get your hands dirty.

*NB Most songs feature a **Roud Number** from the Roud Folk Song Index, created by the remarkable modern folklorist Steve Roud to standardise references to folk songs.*

A Dhomhnaill, a ghràidh mo chridhe This bitter lament that Islay has lost its youth is quoted by John Prebble in *The Highland Clearances,* during his chapter on The White Sailed Ships. I've not found it quoted elsewhere.

All Around My Hat (Roud 22518) This popular English love song, made famous by Steeleye Span in 1975, draws on the habit of wearing green willow sprigs in one's hatband to symbolise mourning. There are many versions. This wording, sung by my colleagues Chris Hayes and Jan North, stems from a cockney music hall broadside from the 1830s. See Mudcat and Mainly Norfolk for a lot of discussion on this song.

Amazing Grace (Roud 5430) This Christian hymn was published in 1779 by clergyman John Newton, who'd long witnessed horrors upon the seas. First pressed into the Royal Navy, Newton later worked in the Atlantic slave trade before a sharp spiritual conversion led him to ordination in the Church of England. We don't know what melody, if any, accompanied the words in his English parish of Olney, but the hymn soon became associated with the Shapenote tune *New Britain* (today's standard tune for it) and spread widely in the US during the early 19th century.

The Birkenhead Drill Taken from Rudyard Kipling's 1893 poem *Soldier an' Sailor too*, a tribute to the Royal Marines.

Blow Boys Blow (Roud 703) A halyard shanty sung on merchant ships while pulling a halyard (rope) which typically raised a sail. Some say this shanty arose in the slave trade and the Congo River, that the 'black sheep' were African slaves and the 'embargo' was the Royal Navy's work to enforce abolition of the slave trade.

The Bristol Bridegroom or *The Ship Carpenter's Love for the Merchant's Daughter* (Roud V24910) Heavily contracted here, this version of the ballad came from a 1791 Irish chapbook (cheap booklet of poetry). It is quoted in Dianne Dugaw, *Warrior Women and Popular Balladry*, 1650-1850, University of Chicago 1996.

By the Hush This title is a corruption of the Irish phrase *Bi i do thost*, which means Be Quiet. Also known as *Paddy's Lamentation*, the song has been collected in Canada and printed as a broadside ballad. As Jeff Warner wrote in the sleevenotes of his album *Long Time*

Travelling, 'The realization that Irish immigrants were essentially drafted off the ships into the Union Army during the Civil War provides the distressing backdrop for this song. General Meagher led the renowned Irish-American 69th Brigade from New York.'

Carrying Nelson Home Copyright MJ O'Connor 12th February 2001. Reproduced with permission. Written by singer Mike O'Connor who explains, 'the song describes a coastal passage from Gibraltar to Portsmouth, starting with backing the foresails to initiate the turn off the outer mole at Gibraltar. The various references are to battles Nelson took part in. The languages of the chorus are those of the main combatants at Trafalgar.'

The Coasts of High Barbary (Roud 134) Based on Child Ballad 285, sung frequently in the UK as *High Barbaree*, this version was popular in America between 1795 and 1815, when Barbary pirates often preyed upon American ships.

Coming Around the Horn (Roud 15539) The text of this typical Gold Rush song appeared in *Put's Original California Songster*, San Francisco, 1854, which suggested the tune *Dearest Mae*, which appeared later in *Minstrel Songs Old and New*, Boston 1882. Quoted in Black & Robertson's *The Gold Rush Song Book*, San Francisco 1940.

Dean Cadalan Samhach Gaelic lullaby, widely sung and recorded. Collected by John Lorne Campbell in Nova Scotia in 1937.

Female Transport (Roud BV1284) Earliest version 1819-1844 in the Bodleian ballad collection, said to be contemporaneous with other famous transportation ballads eg, *Van Diemen's Land* and *Young Henry the Poacher*; this version from *Victorian Street Ballads*, London 1937.

The Flying Cloud (Roud 1802) This version is based on the ballad *William Hollander* as was noted in 1906 for the Greig-Duncan

Collection. For much detail, and opinion, check out the thread on Origins: The Flying Cloud at mudcat.org.

Goodbye My Riley-O Originally from the Gullah: descendants of enslaved Africans who lived in the low country regions of Georgia and South Carolina, including both the coastal plain and the Sea Islands. More information, and a different version of this song, in Lydia Parrish's *Slave Songs of the Georgia Sea Islands*, 1942.

Her Bright Smile Haunts Me Still (Roud 4353) These are the lyrics of the 1864 song written by WT Wrightson & JE Carpenter; there's a lovely version collected by Anne & Frank Warner from Eleazar Tillett and Martha Etheridge in 1951; I first heard it sung by the great Jeff Warner.

I Am a Poor Wayfaring Stranger (Roud 3339) Some ascribe this song to Bishop Richard Allen, born a slave, who formed his first congregation in 1787; it appears as both white hymn and black spiritual during the nineteenth century.

Jim Jones at Botany Bay (Roud 5478) Mainly Norfolk dates this transportation ballad to c1830 as it mentions Jack Donahue, who was shot that year. There's a great version by David Jones, one of my favourite singers, on his album *From England's Shore*.

John Kanaka (Roud 8238) Stan Hugill's *Sea Shanties* 1977 says this halyard shanty is an anglicized polynesian work-song, a rare survivor of that breed, and very popular on mid-19th century American ships.

Mamma Mia Dammi Cento Lire Popular 19th century emigration song from Northern Italy, said to be inspired by the ballad *Maledizione Della Madre*.

Matroos Af-Scheyt First published in 1696 in Amsterdam. Translated here by Martin Cleaver. The song appears on the Dutch early music group Camerata Trajectina's *Van Varen en Vechten, Liederen van de Verenigde Oost-Indische Compagnie*, Globe, 2002.

Mr Tapscott (Roud 616) This version developed from various songs include *Mr Tapscott, Heave Away My Johnnies* and *The Irish Girl*. Often sung to the tune of *New York Gals*.

No More Auction Block for Me (Roud 3348) Spiritual popularised by black regiments during the American Civil War; memorably recorded by Paul Robeson, Odetta and Bob Dylan. A rare spiritual in that it refers specifically to the life of a slave.

The Press Gang (Roud 662) Also known as *The Man-o'-War*. Sung by Ewan MacColl on his 1966 album *Manchester Angel*.

The Scolding Wife (Roud 2132) Origins unknown; listed in the Greig Duncan Collection and *The Singing Island, a collection of English & Scots Folksongs*, compiled by Peggy Seeger and Ewan MacColl.

Shanghai Passage Cicely Fox Smith (1882–1954), from her 1931 collection of sea poems *Sailor's Delight*; I have sought and failed to find the copyright holder of this work but, should further information emerge, will be happy to amend future editions.

The Slave's Lament (Roud 29702) Robert Burns, 1792; recorded widely as a song, particularly by Eliza Carthy 1994 on *Waterson: Carthy* and Coope Boyes & Simpson 2010 on *As If*.

The Slave Ship Ballad (Roud V6025), available in Bodleian Ballads online.

The White Cockade (Roud 191) Taken from the version passed down through the remarkable Copper Family from Sussex, whose Bob Copper sang it for the BBC in 1955. AL Lloyd wrote that the song, 'was a favourite with the peasantry in every part of England but more particularly in the mining districts of the North.'

REFERENCES

Part 1: Taken with Violence

KIDNAPPED

Spirited Away: Peter Williamson, *French and Indian Cruelty: The Life and Curious Adventures of Peter Williamson*, York, 1758; Douglas Skelton, *Indian Peter: The Extraordinary Life and Adventures of Peter Williamson*, Edinburgh, 2004; Robert Louis Stevenson, *Kidnapped*, Cassell, 1886; Don Jordan & Michael Walsh, *White Cargo*, Mainstream Publishing, 2007; Barck & Lefler, *Colonial America*, Macmillan, 1958; J. C. Ballagh, *White Servitude in the Colony of Virginia*, Baltimore, 1895.

Trafficked: Julia Martinez, *La Traite des Jaunes, Trafficking in Women and Children across the China Sea* in *Many Middle Passages* ed. Christopher, Pybus & Rediker, University of California Press, 2007; James Francis Warren, *Ah Ku and Karayuki-san*, NUS Press, 2003; League of Nations, *Commission of Enquiry into Traffic in Women and Children in the East*, 1932; Kevin Bales & Zoe Trodd editors, *To Plead our Own Cause: Personal Stories by Today's Slaves*, Cornell University Press, 2008.

A Flexible Workforce: Jordan & Walsh, *White Cargo*; Barck & Lefler, *Colonial America*; Maryland Gazette, Annapolis, 1745; Bales & Trodd, *To Plead our Own Cause*; runaway advertisement displayed in website, *The Geography of Slavery in Virginia*, www2.vcdh.virginia.edu/gos/.

White Slaves, Barbary Slavers: Des Ekin, *The Stolen Village: Baltimore and the Barbary Pirates*, O'Brien, 2006; Jordan & Walsh,

White Cargo; Giles Milton, *White Gold, the Extraordinary Story of Thomas Pellew and Islam's One Million White Slaves*, Hodder, 2004; Robert C. Davis, *Christian Slaves, Muslim Masters: White Slavery in the Mediterranean, the Barbary Coast, and Italy 1500-1800*, Basingstoke, 2003; Capt Walter Croker, *The Cruelties of the Algerine Pirates*, London, 1816.

ENSLAVED

The Zong: James Walvin, *The Zong: A Massacre, the Law and the End of Slavery*, Yale University Press, 2011; Adam Hochschild, *Bury the Chains*, Macmillan, 2005; Prince Hoare, *Memoirs of Granville Sharp, Esq*, London 1820.

The Loading of the Cargo: Henry Smeathman letter 10th May 1773, Uppsala University Library, quoted in Hochschild, *Bury the Chains*.

Ghost Ships: described in a letter from R. Roddman to H. Chamberlain, Salvador, 12th January 1825, AHI/Notas 284/2/15, quoted in Dale Torston Graden, *From Slavery to Freedom in Brazil: Bahia 1835-1900*, 2006; *The Independent* newspaper, 2nd January 2015.

Olaudah Equiano: David Brion Davis, *Inhuman Bondage: The Rise and Fall of Slavery in the New World*, OUP, 2006; Olaudah Equiano, *The Interesting Narrative of the Life of Olaudah Equiano, or Gustavus Vassa, The African*, 1789; Hochschild, *Bury the Chains*; report on the Guarani tribe appears at survivalinternational.org/tribes/guarani.

Slavery and Song: Ted Gioia, *Work Songs*, Duke University Press, 2006; Stan Hugill, *Shanties from the Seven Seas*, Mystic Seaport Museum Stores, 1961; Joanna C. Colcord, *Songs of American Sailormen*, New York, 1964; David Brion Davis, *Inhuman Bondage*,

OUP 2006; Gad J. Heuman & James Walvin, *The Slavery Reader*, Volume 1, Psychology Press, 2003; Lydia Parrish, *Slave Songs of the Georgia Sea Islands*, 1942.

The Trouble with Tea: James Francis Warren, *Iranun and Balangingi: Globalization, Maritime Raiding and the Birth of Ethnicity*, Singapore University Press, 2002; James Francis Warren, *The Sulu Zone 1768-1898*, Singapore University Press, 1981; William Edwards' handbill quoted in John Falconer, *The Eastern Seas* in David Cordingly ed., *Pirates: An Illustrated History of Privateers, Buccaneers and Pirates from the 16th Century to the Present*, London, 1996; C. Z. Pieters, *Adventures of C. Z. Pieters among the Pirates of Maguindanao*, Journal of the Indian Archipelago and Eastern Asia, 1858; Suey San's story was told by Sam Jones, Guardian newspaper, 16th December 2015; Kate Hodal & Chris Kelly, *Trafficked into slavery on Thai trawlers to catch food for prawns*, Guardian newspaper, 10th June 2014; Kevin Bales, *Disposable People: New Slavery in the Global Economy*, University of California Press, 1999; *Inside the Prawn Slave Trade*, Daily Mail, 14th December 2015; George MacDonald Fraser, *Flashman's Lady*, London, 1977, p168.

Blackbirding: Laurence Brown, *A Most Irregular Traffic, The Oceanic Passages of the Melanesian Labor Trade* in *Many Middle Passages* ed. Christopher, Pybus & Rediker; H.E. Maude, *Slavers in Paradise*, Institute of Pacific Studies, 1981; Hugill, *Shanties from the Seven Seas;* Gioia, *Work Songs*.

Mutiny: Edgar Holden, *'A Chapter on the Coolie Trade'*, Harper's New Monthly Magazine Vol 29, June 1864; Evelyn Hu-deHart, *La Trata Amarilla The 'Yellow Trade' and the Middle Passage, 1847-1884* in *Many Middle Passages* ed. Christopher, Pybus & Rediker; AFP news report, 23rd July 2014.

PRESSED

The British Appetite for Abolition: Nicholas Rogers, *The Press Gang: Naval Impressment and its Opponents in Georgian Britain*, Continuum, 2008; Hochschild, *Bury the Chains*; J.R. Hill, *The Oxford Illustrated History of the Royal Navy*, OUP, 1996.

The Life and Sufferings of James M'Lean: James M'Lean, *Seventeen Years' History of The Life and Sufferings of James M'Lean, An Impressed American Citizen and Seaman*, Hartford, 1814.

CLEARED

Clearance: John Prebble, *The Highland Clearances*, Penguin, 1963; James Hunter, *A Dance Called America, The Scottish Highlands, the United States and Canada*, Edinburgh, 1994; Eric Richards, *The Highland Clearances*, Birlinn, 2013; Billy Kay, *The Scottish World: A Journey Into the Scottish Diaspora*, Mainstream Publishing, 2008; Malcolm Bangor-Jones, *The Assynt Clearances*, The Assynt Press, 2001; report on the killing of Marcos Veron appears at survivalinternational.org/tribes/guarani.

The Slaves Speak Gaelic: Hunter, *A Dance Called America;* Kay, *The Scottish World: A Journey Into the Scottish Diaspora;* John Lorne Campbell, *Songs Remembered in Exile*, Birlinn, 1999; Yale music scholar and jazz musician Willie Ruff's theories on the connection between 18th century Scotland and black gospel music are described in Chuck McCutcheon, *Indian, Black Gospel and Scottish Singing Form an Unusual Musical Bridge*, Washington Post, 21st April 2007.

Le Grand Dérangement: Earle Lockerby, *The Deportation of the Acadians from Ile St.-Jean, 1758*, Acadiensis XXVII, 2 (Spring 1998); George Winslow Barrington, *Remarkable Voyages & Shipwrecks*, London, 1880.

TRANSPORTED

Felons Away: Jordan & Walsh, *White Cargo;* John Lauson, *The poor unhappy transported felon's sorrowful account of his 14 years transportation at Virginia, in America*, 1780; Ballagh, *White Servitude in the Colony of Virginia*.

Jim Jones at Botany Bay: *Bushrangers and Bushranging; or An Old Tale Retold*, The Colac Herald, Victoria, 8th April 1879.

The Women of the First Fleet: *Women Prisoners of the First Fleet*, Letter from Governor Philip to Under Secretary Nepean, 18th March 1787, Historical Records of New South Wales; Arthur Bowes Smyth, *A Journal of a Voyage from Portsmouth to New South Wales and China*, National Library of Australia, 2015.

Reality: This story was reported in the San Jose Mercury News in 1990 and quoted at vietka.com, an archive of Vietnamese boat people maintained by Trinh Hoi.

Part 2: Duped or Desperate

EMIGRATE

Adrift, Adrift: Hashem Alsouki's story appeared in the Guardian newspaper on 9th June 2015 – he succeeded in reaching Sweden; Prebble, *The Highland Clearances*.

The Business of Cargo: Hunter, *A Dance Called America;* Herman Melville, *Redburn: His First Voyage*, New York, 1849; A.R.M. Lower, *Great Britain's Woodyard*, Montreal, 1973; Basil Lubbock, *The Western Ocean Packets*, Boston, 1925; sleeve notes to *Short Sharp Shanties Vol 1*, Kendrick, Brown & Brown, 2011.

Foul Agency: sleeve notes to *Short Sharp Shanties Vol 1*, Kendrick, Brown & Brown, 2011; sleevenotes to Tony Barrand, John Roberts, Jeff Warner et al, *Across the Western Ocean*, 2000; James S Donnelly Jr, *The Great Irish Potato Famine*, Stroud, 2002; Peter Beaumont & Patrick Kingsley, *Devil & the deep blue sea: how the Mediterranean migrant disaster unfolded*, Guardian newspaper, 1st October 2014; *For refugees, the 'trip of death' begins on Egypt's beaches*, Aljazeera America, 17th January 2015; Patrick Kingsley, *Trading in souls; inside the world of the people smugglers*, Guardian newspaper, 7th January 2015.

An Irish Coffin Ship: Robert Whyte, *Ocean Plague, The Diary of a Cabin Passenger*, US, 1847; Donnelly, *The Great Irish Potato Famine*, *Jeanie Johnston* via jeaniejohnston.ie and wikipedia.

Cannibalism Afloat: *White Cargo*, Don Jordan & Michael Walsh; *Pennsylvania Gazette*, 12th November 1741; *Associated Press*, 4th November 2008.

Awful Wreck of an Emigrant Ship: *Armagh Guardian*, 4th June 1849; *Newry Telegraph*, 11th June 1849.

New Scotland: Alexander MacKenzie, *Highland Clearances*, Inverness, 1883; Lucille H. Campey, *After the Hector: The Scottish Pioneers of Nova Scotia and Cape Breton*, Natural Heritage Books, 2004; Prebble, *The Highland Clearances*.

Mediterranean Refugee Disaster: Mark I. Choate, *Emigrant Nation: The Making of Italy Abroad*, Harvard, 2008; Ferruccio Macola, *L'Europa alla conquista dell'America Latina*, Venice, 1894; Claudia Baldoli, *A History of Italy*, Palgrave Macmillan, 2009; Victor R. Greene, *A Singing Ambivalence: American Immigrants Between Old World and New, 1830-1930*, Kent State University Press, 2004.

Hiraeth: Emigration figures from the National Library of Wales; Jonathan Edwards quoted in Alan Edwards ed., *The Welsh in*

America: Letters from the Immigrants, University of Minnesota Press, 1961; Pamela Petro wrote about *hiraeth* on 18th September 2012 in www.theparisreview.org/blog.

Letters from Little England: *The Alderney Press*, Issue 192, 18th September 2015.

VOLUNTEER

The Bounty: Peter Warren Singer, *Children at War*, University of California Press, 2006; *In Syria's war, Alawites pay heavy price for loyalty to Bashar-al-Assad*, Daily Telegraph, 7th April 2015. Chorus quoted from the traditional Scottish song *Twa Recruitin' Sergeants*.

Dying for the Dutch: O. F. Mentzel, *Life at the Cape in Mid-Eighteenth Century: Being the Biography of Rudolf Siegfried Allemann*, Cape Town, 1784, Van Riebeeck Society Reprint, 1919; Nigel Penn, *The Voyage Out*, in *Many Middle Passages* ed. Christopher, Pybus & Rediker; Jaap Jacobs & Hermann Wellenreuther, *Jacob Leisler's Atlantic World in the Later Seventeenth Century*, Lit Verlag, 2010; Georg Fertig, *Transatlantic Migration from the German-Speaking Parts of Central Europe, 1600-1800*, Oxford, 1994.

In Perfect Order as They Drown: James E Wise & Scott Baron, *Soldiers Lost at Sea: A Chronicle of Troopship Disasters*, Naval Institute Pres, 2004; Rudyard Kipling, *Soldier an' Sailor Too*, 1893.

The Union Army Recruits in Ireland: Scott Reynolds Nelson, *After Slavery, Forced Drafts of Irish & Chinese Labor in the American Civil War* in Many Middle Passages ed. Christopher, Pybus & Rediker; sleevenotes to Jeff Warner's *Long Time Travelling*, 2011; *They served their country. Now they can't live in it.*, PBS Newshour, 10th September 2015; *US Army Expands Immigrant Recruitment*

Program, The Wall Street Journal, 8th April 2015; many deported veterans are supported by deportedveteranssupporthouse.org.

OTHER CARGO

The Dockside Crimps: Sleevenotes to Barrand, Roberts, Warner et al, *Across the Western Ocean.*

Rushing for the Gold: James Jupp, *The Australian People: An Encyclopedia of the Nation, Its People and Their Origins*, Cambridge University Press, 2001; Henry Lawson, *In the Days When the World Was Wide*, Sydney, 1900; *The Australian Gold Rush*, from australia.gov.au; *Immigrant Influences – Australian Gold Fields*, from goldrushcolony.com.au; Edwin Bird, *Diary on Marco Polo, Liverpool to Melbourne, 1853*, National Library of Australia ms 6064; Richard A. Dwyer& Richard E. Lingenfelter & David Cohen, *The Songs of the Gold Rush*, University of California Press, 1964.

Final Voyage: Roger Knight, *The Pursuit of Victory, the life and achievement of Horatio Nelson*, Penguin, 2005; may maritime experts forgive me for using two illustrations here which do not feature HMS Victory.

INDEX